Supermarket Backpacker

A collection of lightweight food ideas
for those who choose to search for the simple life
with their homes on their backs.

Supermarket Backpacker

by Harriett Barker

Contemporary Books, Inc.
Chicago

Copyright © 1977 by Harriett Barker
All rights reserved
Published by Contemporary Books, Inc.
180 North Michigan Avenue, Chicago, Illinois 60601
Manufactured in the United States of America
Library of Congress Catalog Card Number: 79-65968
International Standard Book Number: 0-8092-7307-1

Cover design by Paul J. Henderson/St. Louis

Illustrations by Lee Brock and Kent Starr

Contents

Acknowledgments

Dr. Robert Parker, M.D., for his interest and suggestions.

Jan Tasker, Lois Pitzer, Barbara Reznick, John Shannon and
  Sally Cook for sharing their proven ideas and recipes.

Extension Service of Washington State University, Pullman,
  Wash. 99163.

Extension Service of Utah State University, Logan, Utah 84322.

Haiku written especially for this book by Edrie Jefferson, Payson,
  Arizona.

Harriett Barker

Introduction

Because lightweight foods have become so expensive, many back-packers start out with an inadequate haphazard diet they hope will sustain them during the rigors of trail living.

Supermarket shelves are loaded with tasty lightweight foods which take a relatively short time to prepare. Picture yourself at a remote camp when reading label instructions. If it takes too many cooking utensils, or too long to prepare (20 minutes should be absolute maximum) then that is the product to leave on the shelf.

You can easily dry and package your own meals. However, it does require advance planning.

Select a wide variety so your meals will be anticipated instead of booed! Backpack foods need not taste like a soggy cardboard box!

To the Drinkwater Creek Gang

Pointers For Backpackers

- Before leaving home, be sure a responsible person has a copy of your trip plans, stating time you expect to return and area you will be in. This important information could save your life.
- Study trail guides and maps. Local rangers and mountaineering clubs are a good source of information about trail conditions, best routes and expected weather.
- It is a good idea to carry extra clothing and food, sunglasses and hat, first-aid kit, flashlight, topographical map and compass (know how to coordinate them before you leave home), wooden matches in a keep-dry container, a small amount of emergency tinder (pencil shavings or short candle) and a sturdy knife.
- Be honest! Stick strictly to the trail. No cutting across switchbacks. Besides, if you cut, you can't claim the total mileage for that section of trail!
- Remember to apply suntan lotion behind your ears and under your chin when above timberline or crossing sunlit snowfields. The reflection will get cha if you don't cover up!

If you forgot your backpack stove:

- Gather firewood ONLY from dry branches or sticks on the ground. Green wood wastes matches!
- Unless you are an ancient Indian, never build a fire against a vertical rock wall. The smoke leaves an everlasting scar.
- Build fires only on pure soil, or on top of rocks that have a thick padding of that same clean dirt.
- Keep your cooking fires small. Cook the food, not yourself!
- Leave a spotless camp area. Any trash thoughtlessly discarded encourages others to mimic your bad habits.

1

Putting It All Together

. . . White violets crowd
Around discarded beer cans
Not at all shyly . . .

Trial and error experience gained on short hikes is the best way to know approximately what and how much food you will need on an extended backpack trip. Health "insurance" in the form of daily multiple and vitamin C tablets will supplement any unplanned deficiencies in your menu. Include extra food in case of an emergency. This can be dried cooked meat or jerky, dried fruits, hard individually wrapped candies and nuts, or concentrated survival bars.

High-calorie foods include whole wheat cereals, eggs, corn and potatoes, ham, beef or pork, cookies and brownies. Fats and sugars such as butter or margarine and sweet drinks can be used to gain added calories.

Search several markets for foods that are displayed unrefrigerated. Be a label reader! Check the list of contents, the weight, and the amount of time required for preparation. If it takes longer than 15-20 minutes to cook, your stove fuel consumption will be too great on an extended trip.

Don't forget that water is the only thing you can cook really well when backpacking in the high mountains. Main meals planned around instant soups, instant rice, and pre-cooked dried meats and fish will be the most efficient to prepare. Instant hot breakfast cereals and cocoa mixes, again, need only boiling water. Pack a variety to avoid boredom.

Use heavyweight plastic bags (Ziploc) to hold pre-measured dry ingredients such as pancake mixes. Add liquid at camp and mix by hand right in the bag instead of dirtying a pot. Expel as much air as possible before sealing. Don't forget any directions you might need.

If you force or squeeze the air out of plastic bottles and bags before sealing, you create a vacuum. They will be less likely to leak, and will require less room to pack.

Discard boxes when packing food. Repackage such things as flavored gelatins, instant puddings, and macaroni and cheese dinners. Put them in plastic bags so they will not take up extra room. Put the LAST DAY'S meals on the bottom when packing, and try to avoid food repetition from one day to the next.

Fill a small eye dropper vial with concentrated swimming pool chlorine to be used to purify water. One drop to a gallon of water is effective. Stir several times to dissipate the strong taste.

Wash all your cooking gear and plates as they are used, and then quickly scald with boiling water. Don't invite ptomaine poisoning or itinerant animals by leaving unwashed utensils till the next morning. They won't be any easier to wash!

Plastic pill bottles with snap-top lids (available from your doctor or druggist) are handy for carrying dry herbs and spices, vitamin pills, wooden matches, a sewing kit (thread, two needles, two buttons, straight pins, safety pins), or as a container for grated parmesan cheese for the spaghetti dinner.

A piece of heavy-gauge plastic can be used for a "pail." Hold by the four corners to carry water to a pre-dug depression in the dirt or sand. Put rocks on the corners and use for a wash basin or dishpan. Place well away from running water or a lake.

Space-saver cooking is important with a one-burner backpack stove. A double boiler can be used to cook the main dish in the bottom half. The upper half can be used to keep instant rice hot or to warm breads or rehydrate dried fruit. A substitute can be made by turning the pot lid upside down if it is of sufficient depth. Use a foil square for a cover. A foil pie pan also can be used.

A Teflon omelet pan is a versatile cooking utensil. Use it for simmering dinner combinations, warming breads, frying pancakes,

cooking a vegetable and cheese omelet or frying bacon on one half and eggs on the other. It is just the right size for two people.

A Teflon skillet with a folding handle (available in outdoor catalogues) can be covered with an inverted foil pie pan to make a cooking pot. The pie pan will fit inside the skillet for travel. Put a paper towel between them to avoid scratching.

The coffee pot that comes with your cook kit works well as a cooking pot. The size is just right for the backpack stove. A tall one-pound coffee can that fits inside the coffee pot when traveling, can be used for heating water for instant coffee, tea, or bouillon, or to wash the dishes. It also can be used to make brown sugar syrup for pancakes. You may want to shape a pouring spout and add a wire bail. Expect to replace it each time you go on a trip.

A "heat-spreader" or "flame-tamer" placed over your one-burner stove will help distribute heat to the edges of a wider pot. It helps keep such foods as Rice-A-Roni from sticking and burning. It also can serve as a bread toaster.

A rubber spatula for cleaning pots and plates will save on dish-washing water at a "dry" camp. A wooden stirring spoon is light-weight, won't melt or burn your hand, and won't scratch Teflon. A metal or enamel cup can be marked with nail polish on the outside to show liquid measurements.

"Soft" plastic bowls keep foods warm longer after serving, and will hold soup, casserole, or pancakes equally well.

Liquid margarine and cooking oil have an objectionable habit of invading everything. Fold a paper towel several times and wrap around the container lid. Secure with a rubber band, then slip it into a plastic bag for insurance.

Polyester and rayon wipe cloths (Handi-Wipes) are long-wearing and reusable. They dry quickly and take up less space than a bunch of paper towels. Cut them in half and use for washing and drying dishes, as a pot holder, or as a wash cloth for kid clean-up. Wet-strength paper towels (Teri, Tuf 'N Ready) can also be used several times.

"Heavyweight" plastic cutlery and plastic-coated paper plates and bowls are feather light. The cutlery is surprisingly sturdy. The "paper" plates and bowls are handy for a "dry" camp if you can burn them after use. Don't, however, cook over burning plastic.

Baking soda should be an indispensable camping ingredient. Use it as a tooth powder, mouth wash, stomach settler, or body deodorant. Dampened to a paste and covered with a damp cloth, it is a sunburn relief, insect de-itcher, and soothing to cuts and scratches. Rub a little on dampened hands to eliminate fish odors. It is also an effective fire extinguisher.

A satisfactory lightweight pot scrubber can be made from a length of nylon net fastened in the middle with a sturdy wide rubber band. To clean it, undo the rubber band, rinse and hang to dry.

A pair of pliers can often be a "third hand." Use them to work on a balky stove, open stuck fuel bottles, and expecially to handle hot pots.

Half a bar of Fels-Naptha soap is excellent for washing dishes and clothes clean. It is also indispensable for a thorough wash-down if you stumble into poison oak or ivy.

May your outing be an enjoyable and rewarding experience.

2

Breakfast, Quick or Lazy

. . . The bright sun's first rays
Explode in the morning sky
And sleepy eyes . . .

If the morning schedule calls for vigorous activities, avoid a heavy meal. An experienced backpacker will eat lunch all day long.

Hot pre-sweetened lemonade mix, hot Tang grapefruit juice, or hot Start orange juice steeped with a couple of whole cloves will open the most unwilling eyes.

DRINK CRYSTALS

Tang—grapefruit, grape, orange
Start—orange
Wyler's—lemonade, grape, cherry
Borden Breakfast Drink—orange

BREAKFAST LEATHER

Combine in a blender:

1 egg
Fresh fruit [one or a combination]
1/3 cup dry milk
Molasses or honey

Spread on plastic wrap to dry. (See Chapter 7.)

If going extra light appeals to you, and you think you can repeat the same food for almost every meal, try the following recipe. Don't plan to use it for more than a couple of days.

Place these ingredients through a food grinder:

1 pound hulled sunflower seeds
1 pound shelled almonds
1/2 pound shredded coconut
1 pound pitted dates
1/2 pound dried apples
1 pound dried peaches
1/2 pound raisins
1 cup toasted wheat germ
1 small package orange or lemon gelatin

Divide into thirds. Leave one third alone; add ground dried fully cooked ham to one third (sparingly because it is salty); and add ground beef jerky to the rest. Divide into "logs" about the size of your thumb and wrap in foil.

At camp: Eat as is, or crumble the plain ones in hot tea or orange drink to give it a consistency change and different flavor.

Wilson's bacon or meat bar could also be crumbled into a third of the combination in place of the ham or beef jerky.

Hot Cereals

FRUIT AND CINNAMON RICE

At home, combine:

1 1/2 cups Minute Rice
1/2 tsp. cinnamon
1/4 cup raisins (or snipped dry apples, dry peach, pear, pineapple, or banana slices)

At camp: Place rice combination in a sauce pan. Add:

1 1/2 cups water
2 tbls. margarine

Bring to a boil, cover, remove from heat. Allow to steam 5-7 minutes. Serve with liquified dry milk mixed with coffee lightener for better taste.

2 servings.

REGULAR RICE AND RAISINS

In a cooking pot with a tight lid, combine:

2/3 cup regular uncooked rice
1 1/3 cups water
1/2 tsp. salt
1/4 cup raisins (or other chopped dry fruit)

Simmer, covered, 15 minutes. Fluff with a fork, remove from heat, cover and steam another 10 minutes.

2 servings

CORN MEAL MUSH

At home, combine:

1/2 cup corn meal
1/2 tsp. salt

At camp: Place in saucepan. Add 1/2 cup cold water and stir till smooth. Gradually add 1 1/2 cups boiling water, stirring constantly till mixture thickens. Cover and simmer 5 minutes, stirring occasionally.

Variations: Add dried cut-up fruit with the cold water.
          Serve with liquefied dry milk and coffee lightener, or margarine and brown sugar.

2 generous servings

HEARTY OVERNIGHT CEREAL

At home, combine:

1 cup cracked wheat
1 cup rolled oats
1/4 cup wheat germ
1/4 cup brown sugar
1/2 cup chopped dried fruit
1/2 cup raisins

At camp, place the amount of mixture you wish into a cooking pot. (Approximately 1/2 cup per person.) Cover with water and let stand overnight.

In the morning: Simmer, adding water to avoid sticking. Stir occasionally and cook about 10 minutes.

3-4 servings

Instant Cereals

At home: measure instant or quick cooking cereals into portions. Add dry milk, coffee lightener (to improve the taste), raisins or cut-up fruit, and brown or white sugar.

At camp: add boiling water and a dollop of margarine. Proceed according to package instructions.

Variation: for extra energy, add 1/2 tsp. chia seeds (health food store) per serving.

Instant or one-minute cereals such as Cream of Wheat, Quaker Oats, Cream of Rice, or Malt-O-Meal can be "cooked" right in your bowl or cup. Add about 1/3 cup dry milk to the dry cereal, stir, add hot water to desired consistency, stirring as it is added.

Individual instant oatmeal packets, when opened carefully, will hold the addition of 2 rounded teaspoons of coffee lightener. Reseal with tape. At camp: put in a cup and add hot water.

Breakfast Bars, Granola Bars, and instant breakfast mixes are handy to use if you wish to get an early, easy start.

When measuring dry cereals for two portions, use the amount suggested for four servings if cereal is to be your entire breakfast.

Quick-cook cereals include:

> Cream of Wheat . . . instant, 1/2 minute, or five minutes to cook.
> Cream of Rice . . . 1/2 minute to cook.
> Malt-O-Meal . . . one minute to cook.
> Quick Quaker Oats . . . one minute to cook.
> Wheat Hearts . . . 3-5 minutes to cook.
> Wheatena . . . 5 minutes to cook.
> Ralston . . . 5 minutes to cook.
> Roman Meal . . . 5 minutes to cook.
> Zoom . . . 5 minutes to cook.
> Quick Grits . . . 5 minutes to cook.
> White Corn Meal . . . 5 minutes to cook.

Flavor bland cereals like oatmeal or Cream of Wheat with:
Dried Fruits—Chopped apricots, dates, prunes, raisins, apples, banana slices, pineapple, coconut, etc.
Flavors—Instant chocolate drink mix, carob powder (health store) cinnamon or nutmeg, orange or grape drink crystals, flavored gelatins, peanut butter, assorted chopped nuts, leathered apple sauce, fruit leathers, chia or sunflower seeds.
Sweeteners—Miniature marshmallows, brown or white sugar, honey, crushed peppermint sticks, soft mints, chocolate bar, butterscotch bits.

Bran cereals such as Bran Buds and All-Bran, and Wheatena cooked cereal are important for their food fiber content to help establish regularity. Flax seed is also helpful. It can be found in Uncle Sam Dry Cereal.

For a change, combine quick-cooking cereals that require the same cooking time. Roman Meal with Oatmeal, and Wheat Hearts with Cream of Wheat are both good. This will serve two:

At home, combine: **1/2 cup Roman Meal Quick Cooking Cereal**
 1/2 cup Quaker Quick Oatmeal
 1/2 cup dry milk
 1/2 tsp. salt

At camp: stir cereal into 2 cups water. Bring to a boil, cover, and remove from heat. Let stand five minutes.

Serve with coffee lightener mixed with hot water, some margarine, and sugar.

Granolas

Serve this over granola:

STEWED FRUIT COMPOTE

At home, combine:

      6 oz. (approx.) dried fruit, cut up small
      1/4 cup raisins
      2 tbls. brown sugar
      1/2 tsp. cinnamon or nutmeg
      1/3 cup shredded coconut

At camp: Place in a sauce pan. Cover with water and simmer 10-15 minutes or till fruit is plump. Serve as is, or spooned over your favorite granola.

2-3 servings

GRANOLA VARIATIONS

Even if you plan to have granola for every breakfast, you can have a different taste by dividing plain granola into portions. To each individual portion add 1/3 cup dry milk, 2 tbls. coffee lightener, then include:

> chopped dates
> raisins
> cut up figs that have been rolled in powdered sugar
> coconut shreds
> dry roasted sunflower or pumpkin seeds
> piñon nuts
> a sprinkle of flavored gelatin

At camp, top with hot or cold water.

HOME-MADE GRANOLA

(Proportions are not important)

Combine: Grape Nuts
           Bran Buds
           Rice or Wheat Puffs
           Rice or Wheat Chex
           Buc-Wheats
Add: brown sugar
           sesame seeds
           coconut
           chopped nuts (walnuts, almonds, etc.)
           toasted wheat germ

Sprinkle with 1 tsp. vanilla. Drizzle with honey. Stir well and spread on a rimmed cookie sheet. Place in a 350° oven for 15 minutes, stirring every 5 minutes. Cool and store airtight in refrigerator or freezer if not to be used right away.

A BETTER GRANOLA

At home, combine:

3 cups rolled oats
2 cups each wheat germ, Grape Nuts, shredded coconut
1 cup each hulled sunflower seeds, chopped nuts.

Heat together till runny: 1 cup honey, 2 tsp. vanilla (do not cook).
   Add to dry mixture and stir thoroughly. Spread in shallow pans and place in a 325° oven for 20 minutes or till browned. Stir often.
   When cool, add chopped dried fruit of your choice. Use as a snack or with milk.

This is a delicious breakfast or trail snack:

WHOLE WHEAT NUTS

Combine:

3 cups whole wheat flour
2 tsp. baking soda
1 cup packed brown sugar
1 tsp. salt
1 cup buttermilk

Mix thoroughly and put in a greased 9" x 13" baking pan. Bake at 300° until golden brown, approximately 45 minutes.
   Crumble into small pieces and dry thoroughly.(See chapter on drying.)

Breakfasts You Can Drink

Use a container with a tight lid for mixing the following individual proportions. Whole fresh eggs may be substituted for dry egg powder.

ORANGE BREAKFAST

At camp, add 1 cup water to:
> **1/3 cup dry milk**
> **1-2 tbls. orange crystals (Start, Tang)**
> **1 tbls. brown sugar**
> **1 heaping tbls. dry egg powder**

GRAPEFRUIT BREAKFAST

At camp, add 1 cup water to:
> **1 heaping tbls. dry egg powder**
> **1-2 tbls. grapefruit crystals (Tang)**
> **1 tbls. honey**

GRAPE BREAKFAST

At camp, add 1 cup water to:
>**1 heaping tbls. dry egg powder**
>**2 tbls. coffee lightener**
>**1/3 cup dry milk**
>**1-2 tbls. grape crystals**

BREAKFAST NOG

At camp, add 1 cup water to:
>**1 heaping tbls. dry egg powder**
>**1/3 cup dry milk**
>**Dash of cinnamon or nutmeg**
>**1 tsp. brown or white sugar**

>*Variation:* Add crushed dry banana or strawberry slices.

FRUIT NOG

At camp, add 1 cup water to:
>**1 heaping tbls. dry egg powder**
>**Syrup drained from stewed fruit (apple, prune, etc.)**

MOCHA NOG

At camp, add 1 cup water to:
1 heaping tbls. dry egg powder
1/3 cup dry milk
1 tbls. coffee lightener
1 tsp. instant coffee

CHOCOLATE NOG

At camp, add 1 cup water to:
1 heaping tbls. dry egg powder
1/3 cup dry milk
1 tbls. coffee lightener
2 heaping tsp. hot cocoa mix

BREAKFAST BOUILLON

Combine thoroughly: **1 heaping tbls. dry egg powder**
1 tsp. instant bouillon (chicken,
beef, onion)

Add a few drops of cold water and stir to make a smooth paste. Add hot water and stir till dissolved.

Make a "creamed bouillon" by adding dry milk or coffee lightener, and a dollop of margarine.

Top with croutons and parmesan cheese.

1 serving

BACON IDEAS

Bacon slices are messy to handle, and become strong tasting in a few days without refrigeration. However, if you do choose to carry bacon, take a metal baking powder can with a plastic lid (Calumet). It will safely contain cooled congealed grease you can use later for flavoring pancakes, eggs and vegetables. Slip the can into a sturdy plastic bag (Ziploc) for insurance.

Canadian bacon keeps better and is not as messy as regular bacon. You can also use your own dried ham bits (see chapter on drying), Wilson's Bits 'O Bacon, Wilson's concentrated Bacon Bar (available in outdoor shops and catalogues), or one of the textured vegetable protein (t.v.p.) substitutes.

Following is a method of preparing bacon that helps eliminate chances of spoiling on a long trip:

Cover separated bacon strips with water and bring to a boil for 30 seconds. Dry on a paper towel. Dip in corn meal, then fry crisp. Use crumbled in omelets, pancake batter, and as a vegetable garnish.

Fresh Eggs

Nature provides an excellent natural container for fresh eggs which protects the nutrients as long as the shell and membrane are intact. Medium and small eggs are easier to pack, and generally have more sturdy shells.

If packed in a quart milk carton, eggs can be cushioned with popped corn or instant rice. Keep the cartons cool in the nearest lake or stream when camped.

For nourishing, easily prepared meals, add dried soup mixes, instant bouillon, cheese, or bacon bits to eggs.

Soft-boil breakfast eggs in your instant coffee water. Add the fresh eggs *before* the water comes to a boil to avoid cracking.

Scrambled Egg Variations

Mix with a fork:
> **4 eggs**
> **2 tbls. dry milk**
> **4 tbls. water**
> **1/2 tsp. salt, dash of pepper**

Add one of the following:
> **4 tbls. shredded cheddar, Jack or Swiss cheese**
> **4 tbls. rehydrated mushroom pieces**
> **1 tbls. crushed dry parsley or celery leaves**
> **1 tbls. bacon bar (Wilson's)**
> **3 tbls. rinsed shredded dried beef**
> **1/2 tsp. chili powder**
> **1 tbls. dried tomato slices, crushed**

Powdered Dry Eggs

Powdered dry eggs are ideal for backpacking. They can be scrambled for breakfast, mixed with the dry ingredients of pancakes, or combined in sauces for easy nourishing food preparation. Refrigeration is not necessary. Write to the following companies for information:

A.J. Pietrus and Sons, Co.
Sleepy Eye, Minnesota 56085

Their product is called "Nutri-Egg." It keeps indefinitely on the shelf, and comes in 20-oz. cans with plastic snap-on lids.

Marshall Produce Co.
P.O. Box 1088
Marshall, Minn. 56258

They make E-Z Egg Mix. One packet is equivalent to a dozen shelled eggs.

Though flavorful when mixed according to directions, dry egg powder mixes readily with dry herbs, grated cheeses, and rehydrated meats and vegetables for a quick meal.

SCRAMBLED EGGS AND CHEESE

Combine with a wire whip or fork:

2/3 cup dry egg powder
1 tbls. wheat germ
3 tbls. dry milk
Pinch of dry parsley, salt and pepper
2/3 cup lukewarm water

Melt 2 tbls. margarine in a frying pan. Add egg mixture.

Top with shredded Swiss, Jack or cheddar cheese. Stir lightly and cook to your liking.

2 servings

Pancakes from Scratch or Mix

Pancake Mix Additions:

Quick cooking cereals (Roman Meal, Oatmeal, Ralston)
Coconut shreds
Chopped nuts (walnuts, almonds, peanuts)
Sunflower seeds, piñon nuts, chia seeds (health food store)
Orange drink crystals (Tang, Start)
Flavored gelatins or puddings
Crunchy peanut butter
Baco-Bits, Bits 'O Bacon (seasoning section of market)
Washed, cut-up dandelion blossoms, wild rose petals, wild violets
Dried low-fat cottage cheese (see chapter on drying)
Dry banana or apple slices
Dry apple peel
Chocolate or butterscotch bits

Use a corn muffin mix (Cinch, Jiffy, Dromedary) and add more liquid to make tasty pancakes.

Fruit muffin mixes can also be used to make pancakes. Be sure the frying pan is well greased, and add melted margarine to the batter.

Place the dry ingredients in a Ziploc bag. *At camp,* add the liquids to the bag and squeeze by hand to mix. Pour right from the bag to bake. No messy clean-up!

GRANOLA PANCAKES

At home, combine:

3/4 cup granola cereal
1 cup whole wheat flour
1-3/4 cup all-purpose flour
1 tsp. salt
2 tsp. baking powder
2/3 cup dry milk
1/3 cup dry egg powder
2 tbls. brown sugar

At camp: Add water to make a thin batter. Melt 3 tbls. margarine and add to the batter. Fry on a greased frying pan.

8-10 cakes

WHEAT PANCAKES

At home, combine:

1 heaping tbls. egg powder
1/3 cup dry buttermilk powder (Darigold Brand)
3/4 cup whole wheat flour
1 tbls. brown sugar
1 tsp. baking powder
1/2 tsp. soda
1/2 tsp. salt

At camp, add: **1 cup water**
2 tbls. melted margarine

Bake in a greased frying pan.

8-10 cakes

WHEAT GERM AND APPLE PANCAKES

At home, combine:

3/4 cup whole wheat flour
3/4 cup all-purpose flour
2 tbls. wheat germ
3 tsp. baking powder
1/2 tsp. salt
1/2 tsp. cinnamon
1/3 cup dry egg powder
1 tbls. brown sugar
2/3 cup dry milk
1/2 cup dried apple slices, cut up

At camp: Melt 4 tbls. margarine in a frying pan. Add enough water to make a thin batter. Add melted margarine. Fry in a greased pan.

8-10 cakes

CORN PANCAKES

At home, combine:
1/2 cup dry milk
1/2 cup cornmeal
3/4 cup flour (unbleached if available)
1/2 tsp. salt
2 tsp. baking powder
2 heaping tbls. dried egg powder

At camp: Add 1-1/4 cups water and 2 tbls. melted margarine. Bake in a greased frying pan. Add bacon to batter, if desired.
6-8 cakes

BUTTERMILK CORN CAKES

At home, combine:
1/2 cup corn meal
1/2 cup flour (unbleached if available)
1/4 cup wheat germ
1/2 cup dry buttermilk powder (Darigold brand)
1/2 tsp. soda, 1/2 tsp. salt
2 heaping tbls. dry egg powder.

At camp: Add approximately 3/4 cup water to make a thin batter. Melt 1 tbls. margarine or bacon fat and add to batter. Fry in a greased pan.

ORANGE PANCAKES

At home, combine:
1 cup whole wheat flour
1/4 tsp. soda
1/4 tsp. salt
1 heaping tbls. dry egg powder
1 tbls. orange juice crystals (Tang, Start)

At camp: Add 2 tbls. melted margarine and enough water to make a thin batter. For added nutrition, top the unbaked side with hulled sunflower seeds before turning to brown the other side.
1 serving

GRAHAM CRACKER PANCAKES

At home, combine:

> **3/4 cup graham cracker crumbs**
> **3/4 cup whole wheat flour**
> **1/2 cup dry milk**
> **1 tsp. ground cinnamon**
> **2 tsp. baking powder**
> **1/2 tsp. salt**
> **1/3 cup dry egg powder**

At camp, add:

> **1-1/4 cup water**
> **3 tbls. melted margarine**

Combine thoroughly and fry by spoonfuls on a hot greased frying pan.

8-10 cakes

PANCAKES FOR A CROWD

At home, combine:

> **2 cups whole wheat flour**
> **2/3 cup soy flour (health food store)**
> **1-1/2 tsp. salt**
> **6 tsp. baking powder**
> **1 cup dry milk**
> **2/3 cup dry egg powder**
> **1/4 cup brown sugar, packed**
> **1 cup chopped nuts**

At camp, add: 1/4 cup melted margarine and enough water to make a thin batter. Bake on a greased frying pan.

24 4-inch pancakes

Pancake Toppings

Combine margarine with powdered, brown, or white sugar, dash cinnamon.

Cinnamon sugar.

Stewed fruit and juice.

Applesauce spiced with cinnamon candies (Red Hots).

Jam or fruit preserves.

Wild strawberries, blueberries, salmonberries, raspberries, blackberries.

Fruit leather soaked in a small amount of water.
Combine in a saucepan:

> **1/2 cup fruit jelly (apple, grape, mint)**
> **2 tbls. margarine**

Stir over low heat till smooth and jelly is melted.

SYRUP: **1/2 cup white sugar**
> **1/2 cup brown sugar**
> **1/2 cup water**

Simmer till sugar is dissolved.

FRENCH TOAST

At home, combine:

> **1/4 cup flour**
> **1 tbls. sugar**
> **1 cup dry milk**
> **1/2 cup dry egg powder**

At camp: Add 1 cup water and 1 tbls. melted margarine. Dip thick slices of French bread in the mixture. Fry, browning both sides.

8-9 slices

BREAKFAST SANDWICHES

For each sandwich:

- Spread one side of a slice of bread with margarine and place spread side down in a warming frying pan.
- Top with thin slices of fresh apple (or rehydrated stewed apple).
- Sprinkle with bacon bar, Bits 'O Bacon or dried ham bits.
- Add slices of sharp cheese.

Top with a slice of bread that has been spread with margarine. Brown both sides of the sandwich.

Variation: Warm pita bread (pocket bread) and stuff with these same ingredients.

French bread and English muffins toast easily by buttering one side and placing spread side down in a hot skillet.

3

Munch Stop:
On-The-Trail Snacks

. . . It's all here to read—
The secrets of ages past
In this weathered cliff . . .

Snacks are very important on a backpack trip. They help keep your body and mind from slowing down, and assist in retaining your resistance to cold. Plan high-calorie foods such as dried fruits, seeds, nuts, cheese, chocolate, hard candies, malt balls, cookies, dried meat (jerky and ham bits). Concentrated mince meat (Borden brand) makes an excellent snack, but be sure to drink plenty of water with it. It is meant to swell when dampened.

It is often quoted, "An experienced backpacker eats all day." Food is essential for safety as well as gastronomic enjoyment.

Gorp

Gorp is a high-calorie snack. It can be as simple a combination as raisins and *salted* nuts. The salt is important to help you avoid dehydration. To that you can add M and M's, coconut or banana flakes, pumpkin or sunflower seeds, piñon nuts, dried apple slices. The list can be almost endless.

HAWAIIAN GORP

At home, combine in a heavy frying pan:
> **1/2 cup raisins**
> **1/2 cup salted toasted coconut chips**
> **1/2 cup salted roasted peanuts**
> **1/2 cup salted roasted cashews**
> **1 tsp. curry powder**

Stir over low heat 8-10 minutes or till coconut turns yellow.
Variation: Instead of curry powder, use oregano or marjoram.

CHEWY GORP

At home, combine in the top of a double boiler:
> **2 large packages chocolate or butterscotch bits [24 oz.]**
> **1/2 cup honey**

When melted, pour over the following ingredients which you have
assembled in a large bowl:
> **1/2 cup of each of the following: — chopped dates,**
> **raisins, dried chopped apples, shredded coconut,**
> **chopped almonds, chopped walnuts, wheat germ,**
> **uncooked quick oatmeal, granola.**
> **Also add 2 tbls. chia seeds**

Mix well. Pour into greased pans, press firmly and cool. Cut or
break into small chunks.

CALORIE BALLS
PEANUT BUTTER BALLS

At home, combine:
> **1/2 cup smooth peanut butter**
> **1/2 cup honey**

Gradually add and stir in:
> **1 cup dry milk**
> **1 cup uncooked "quick" oatmeal**

Measure portions with a melon baller or teaspoon. Shape into balls. Place on a plate or waxed paper to "dry" for several hours.
> *Variation:* Use any quick-cooking cereal.
> Roll balls in toasted wheat germ.

ALL-IN-ONE BALLS

At home, combine in a double boiler:
> **1 pound crunchy peanut butter**
> **8 ounces honey**

Pour this mixture over:
> **1/4 cup powdered yeast**
> **1/4 cup sesame seeds**
> **1/4 cup chia seeds**
> **1/4 cup wheat germ**
> **1/4 cup raisins**
> **1/4 cup chopped apples (dried)**
> **1/4 cup dry milk**
> **1 cup mixed chopped nuts**
> **1 tbls. molasses**
> **Salt to taste**

Form into balls and roll in toasted wheat germ or fine ground coconut. Add sharp cheese and a hot drink for a simple meal.

GRAIN BALLS

At home, combine:

> **1 cup each: whole wheat flour, corn meal, rice flour
> (health food store), cooked brown or regular rice,
> cooked bulgur or cracked wheat, cooked millet.**

Add: **Salt to taste**

Shape into 1″ balls. Roll in granulated or powdered sugar. Bake at
400° for 10 minutes or till crusty on the outside.

HERBED MUSHROOMS (a salty snack)

Clean and slice one pound of fresh mushrooms about 1/4″ thick.
Place in a roomy bowl. Combine:

> **1/4 tsp. each garlic and onion salt**
> **1/2 tsp. salt**
> **1/2 tsp. each oregano and thyme**

Sprinkle seasonings over mushroom slices and carefully stir with a
rubber spatula. Use a vegetable cooking spray to coat two cookie
sheets. Spread mushroom slices so as not to overlap. Dry till crisp.
(See chapter on drying.)

Corn

Long-distance runners of the Tarahumara Indian tribe living in the high mountains of Mexico subsist on *pinole* during traditional stick-and-ball games that last as long as 72 hours.

PINOLE

Grind white unseasoned popped corn as fine as possible in a food grinder or blender. Add sugar and dry milk according to your taste. To use: add to water to make a hot or cold drink; sprinkle over hot or cold cereals; as coating for sticky fruits.

PARCHED CORN

Choose mature ears of corn. Peel back the husks and hang to dry in a warm, dry spot. When the kernels are easily rubbed from the cob, remove them and blow away the small husks.

Use a large cast-iron frying pan or heavy Dutch oven (aluminum or iron). Coat very lightly with cooking oil and wipe with a paper towel. Place over medium heat. Add a layer of dry corn. Stir continually. A wire whip works well. The kernels will expand and snap, sometimes hopping right out of the pan.

When snapping has stopped and the kernels are shiny, remove from heat and spread on paper towels to cool. Add salt if desired.

Use for energy in the gorp bag, add to soups or stews for crunch, or grind fine and add to pancake mix or use as a thickener for stews, etc.

Nuts and Seeds

Nuts and seeds contain fat and protein which make them a valuable and sustaining food.

To blanch almonds or walnuts: drop the shelled nut into boiling water, remove from heat and let stand 5 minutes. Drain, slip off the skins and blot dry with paper towels or a thick turkish towel. Dry thoroughly before storing. (See chapter on drying foods.)

Buy unshelled sunflower seeds at a pet shop. They are usually larger and much less expensive than those found in markets. Roast your own.

OVEN-FLAVORED NUTS

Roasting and flavoring fresh raw nuts and seeds is a simple matter of heating them with a little oil and seasonings.

Spread a layer of shelled nuts in a shallow pan. Bake at 350°.
Allow 8-10 minutes for pine nuts, peanuts, pecans, blanched almonds, blanched walnuts and sunflower seeds.
Allow 15 minutes for hazelnuts, filberts, cashews.
Allow 40 minutes for rinsed cleaned fresh pumpkin and squash seeds. Stir every five minutes.
Dump heated nuts into a generous bowl. Sprinkle with 1-2 tsp. salad oil or melted margarine, and sprinkle with a seasoning (garlic salt, onion salt, regular salt, paprika, chili powder, smoke-flavored salt, parmesan cheese). Stir to coat seeds, return to baking pan and place back in the oven for 2-3 minutes, stirring several times. Cool and store airtight in glass jars in a cool place.

Dried Fruits

Even *pitted* prunes are heavy. Use them in a combination with lighter weight fruits.

CANDIED CITRUS PEEL

At home: wash, peel and cut the rind of one large grapefruit in half-inch-wide strips. Place in a saucepan and cover with cold water. Heat to boiling and boil for five minutes. Drain.

Repeat three times. Boil in a fourth water till tender, drain and place in a fifth water. Add 1 cup sugar to each cup of cooked rind. Boil until the mixture becomes syrupy and thick. Drain and roll in granulated sugar. Place on waxed paper to dry.

Orange Candied Peel: Use four large navel oranges. Boil the strips of peel in three changes of water instead of five. Proceed as for grapefruit.

STUFFED DRIED FRUITS

Use pitted dates, prunes, peaches, pears or apricots to stuff. Insert whole nuts or cheese cubes. Combine 1/4 cup peanut butter with powdered sugar to make a stiff paste. Use in dates or prunes.

Mix powdered sugar and molasses for pears; powdered sugar and honey for apricots; powdered sugar and dark Karo syrup for peaches; brown sugar and cinnamon for apples.

Fruit Logs

Flavored gelatin can be used as a sweetener for dried fruit logs. Try cherry or lemon.

SIMPLE FRUIT LOGS

Combine: Dates, raisins, cashews. Force through a food grinder using a medium blade. Shape into logs about the size of your thumb. Wrap individually in foil squares.

FRUIT ROLL #1

Put the following ingredients through a food grinder three times:
   1 pound dried pitted dates
   4 oz. each dried apples, pitted prunes, raisins, candied
      fruit-cake fruit
   4 tbls. flaked coconut
   1 cup mixed salted nuts
   2 tbls. flavored gelatin (cherry or strawberry)
Shape into logs and roll in wheat germ. Let set to "dry." Wrap individually in foil squares.

FRUIT ROLL #2

Using the same method combine:
   1 cup packed pitted prunes which have been cooked 10
      minutes and drained
   1 cup dried figs, and 1 cup raisins
   1/2 cup walnuts or almonds, or both
Shape and roll in toasted coconut that has been chopped fine in a blender.

Energy Bars

(Prepare at Home)
SEED BARS

1/4 cup margarine
3 cups granola cereal
3/4 cup salted sunflower seeds
1 can (14 oz.) sweetened condensed milk

Melt margarine in a 9 x 13 x 2" baking pan. Spread to coat the bottom. Place on a flat surface. Sprinkle granola evenly over margarine. Bake at 325° for 15 minutes. Sprinkle sunflower seeds over granola, and top with the canned milk. Bake 325° for 20 minutes or till browned. Loosen edges. Cool. Cut into small bars. Wrap individually in foil.

PROTEIN BARS

2 tbls. margarine
2 cups miniature marshmallows
2 tbls. peanut butter
1/2 cup chocolate or butterscotch morsels
4 cups high protein cereal (Cheerios or other)

In a double boiler, combine margarine, marshmallows, peanut butter and morsels of your choice. Stir till smooth. Add cereal and mix well. Press into an 8 x 8 x 2" square pan that has been lined with foil. Cool and cut into bars. Lift from pan. Wrap individually in small squares of foil.

Variation: add chopped nuts if desired.

PEANUT BUTTER BARS

1 pkg. (6 oz.) butterscotch morsels
1/3 cup crunchy peanut butter
2 tbls. margarine
3 cups miniature marshmallows
1/4 tsp. salt

In a double boiler combine morsels, peanut butter, margarine, marshmallows and salt. Stir till smooth.

Combine: 2-1/2 quarts of *popped* corn and 1 cup granola cereal. Add the warm peanut butter mixture. Press into a foil-lined pan, 9 x 13 x 2". Cool until firm. Lift from pan. Cut into bars. Wrap in foil and store in a cool place till needed.

FRUIT ENERGY BARS

2 cups crushed vanilla wafers
1/2 cup chopped dates
1/2 cup dried apples, snipped
1 cup raisins
1 cup finely chopped nuts
2 tbls. chia seeds
2/3 cup honey

Combine all ingredients, using enough water to bind the ingredients. Shape into bars. Roll in granulated or powdered sugar, and wrap in foil. Store in a plastic bag in refrigerator or freezer.

Variation: Use 1/3 cup each honey and molasses instead of all honey.

Backpack Breads

(Prepare at Home)

CORN SQUARES

1 8 oz. pkg. corn muffin mix
1 cup chopped salted peanuts
1/2 cup grated parmesan cheese
1 tsp. garlic salt
3 tbls. melted margarine

Prepare muffin mix according to package directions. Spread in a well greased 15 x 10 x 1" jelly roll pan. Sprinkle evenly with peanuts, cheese, garlic salt. Drizzle with melted margarine. Bake at 375° for 25 minutes or till light brown. Cut into squares, cool five minutes, remove and place on cake racks to cool.

Variation: instead of peanuts use toasted sunflower seeds, 1/4 cup chia seeds, or sprinkle with all-bran cereal.

BACKPACKER'S RUSK

Combine: **1 cup whole wheat flour**
          1/2 cup honey

Drop by spoonfuls on a greased cookie sheet. Bake at 350° about 15 minutes or till browned. Cool on racks.

    Variation: Use rye flour and molasses. Use unbleached flour and Karo syrup.

CONDENSED TRAIL BREAD

This is a very firm bread rich in protein and carbohydrates. It keeps well for weeks. Combine thoroughly:
      2 cups unbleached white flour
      2 cups whole wheat flour
      1/3 cup wheat germ
      1/4 cup sesame seed
      3 tbls. dry milk
      3/4 cup packed brown sugar
      1-1/2 tsp. baking powder
      1-1/2 tsp. salt
Combine and add:
      1 cup water
      1/2 cup honey
      1/4 cup molasses
      1/3 cup cooking oil

Stir till smooth and all ingredients are moist. Pour into well greased 8 x 8 x 2″ baking pan. Bake at 300° for one hour. The bread should pull away from the sides of the pan. Cut into small squares while warm. Leave in the pan uncovered for 8-10 hours to dry. Wrap tightly in plastic wrap and store in Ziploc plastic bags.

Peanut Butters

HOMEMADE PEANUT BUTTER

Place 1-1/2 cups salted peanuts in a blender. Cover and process, pushing ingredients into the blades occasionally.

Variations: Add crisp cooked bacon, fresh apple, orange peel (sparingly), marmalade, dried fruit such as raisins, dates, honey, or fruit jelly. Make a peanut butter spread by adding a generous amount of margarine to the ground peanuts.

BEEF JERKY

Jerky is best when dried in the hot sun, but this method doesn't require you to bring it in at night to avoid absorbing dew.

1 lean flank steak (any lean beef is suitable)
partially frozen so it will slice easier
Marinade:
1/2 cup soy sauce
1/4 cup Worcestershire sauce
1/4 tsp. each garlic, onion, regular salt

Cut rolled steak into strips 3/8" to 1/2" wide. Trim away all fat. Lay strips flat in a jelly roll pan. Place a second layer going the opposite way for ease in handling. Combine marinade and pour over the meat strips, moving them around so the marinade comes in contact with all of them. Cover with plastic wrap, pressing it down on the meat to remove air pockets. Refrigerate overnight.

Next morning: Stretch *washed* nylon net or cheesecloth tightly over oven racks. Fasten with safety pins or clothes pins. Blot the marinade from the meat with paper towels and place strips on racks *not* touching. Keep the top oven rack at least five-inches from the light bulb.

Replace the oven light with a 150-watt bulb. Prop the oven door open slightly to allow moisture to escape. A folded paper towel or hot pad will work well. Protect the meat nearest the light with a paper towel. Rotate the trays often for even drying.

Beef jerky should be pliable when ready. Store in Ziploc plastic bags or tightly covered glass jars till ready to use.

PEMMICAN

Indian pemmican was mostly fruit and fat. Early Americans made a pemmican of jerky, fat, raisins and sugar. Modern pemmican comes close to being a fully nutritious food. It is compact, tasty, and keeps well for at least a month. A basic non-meat pemmican includes the following categories and suggestions:

SEEDS—sunflower, chia, pumpkin

NUTS—almond, peanut, walnut, etc. or parched corn
         (see index)

FRUITS—dried pitted dates, pitted prunes, raisins, currants,
         figs, apricots, apples, etc.

Add: wheat germ, salt, dry milk powder, unflavored gelatin powder, carob powder.

Put your selection of ingredients through a food grinder set at "coarse." Shape into thumb-size "logs." Wrap individually in foil or plastic wrap squares.

Meat pemmican is composed of shredded jerky, bacon or meat bar from an outdoor shop, or very dry salami with very little fat in it. The meat is added to the seed, nut, fruit combination.

4

Lunch Stop:
Time to Take Time Out

. . . The visiting wind
Gossips with that swaying tree
And a rolling can . . .

LUNCH SUGGESTIONS: Choose bread and crackers that are sturdy
and compact.
Bread: Party rye, pumpernickel, bagels, sourdough French
bread, pita (pocket) bread, English muffins.
Crackers: Rye wafers (Knachbrod, Ry Krisp), Wheat Thins,
Stoned Wheat Wafers, Roman Meal Wafers, Pilot bread,
Waverly's, graham crackers.
Meats: Dry salami, smoked meat sticks, beef jerky, dried
cooked ham cubes, dried cooked chicken cubes, dried
cooked lean beef, canned meat spreads.
Cheese: Cheddar, Swiss, Jack, Gouda, Edam, Armenian string
cheese, Swiss gruyere in small wrapped wedges.
Nuts: Your choice, salted preferred to help replace body salts.
Dried fruits: Pitted prunes and dates, figs, raisins, peaches,
apples, apricots, pineapple, pears, banana slices.
Cookies: Chewy compact ones like fig newtons, oatmeal, or
shortbreads.

Candy: Hard individually wrapped butterscotch or fruit drops, lemon drops, peppermints, small chocolate bars, jelly beans, Life Savers, etc.

Variety: Coconut chips, salted unhulled sunflower seeds, salted soy beans, chewing gum.

Cheese

Cheese is the backpacker's alternative to fresh meat. Since it is made from concentrated milk, it is an excellent source of protein and calcium. A quarter pound of cheese is equal in protein and calcium to 4 oz. of lean beef.

Cheese with a wax covering such as Tillamook Cheddar (Baby Loaf or Snack Bar size), Edam, Gouda, and Danish cheeses are less oily and messy. Foil-wrapped cheddar cheese like Kraft's Cracker Barrel variety keep well. The light mild cheeses such as Jack and Swiss varieties will get oily, but are good to add to soups and main dishes. String cheese and Kraft Squeez-a-Snak cheese are good on breads or crackers.

Processed cheese is too oily and sticky to carry. A cheese store will be glad to help you choose varieties that will be best suited for your trip.

CHEESE COINS

Thoroughly combine:
> **1/2 cup margarine**
> **2 cups shredded sharp cheddar cheese**
> **1/2 tsp. Worcestershire sauce**

Add: **1 cup flour, a little at a time. Knead till smooth**

Form into a long roll approximately one inch in diameter. Cut into 1/4" slices with a sharp thin knife, or cheese slicer. Bake at 350° for 12-15 minutes.

Variations: Add 1 tsp. sesame seed, 1/2 tsp. chia seeds, or poppy seeds.

Quick Breads
(Prepare at Home)
CRANBERRY NUT BREAD

Sift together:
>**2 cups all-purpose flour**
>**1/2 cup each white and brown sugar**
>**1-1/2 tsp. baking powder**
>**1 tsp. salt**
>**1/2 tsp. soda**

Cut in: **1/4 cup shortening**

Add: **1 tsp. grated orange peel**
>**1 tbls. chia seeds***
>**3/4 cup orange juice**
>**1 well-beaten egg**

Fold in:
>**1 cup fresh coarsely chopped cranberries**
>**1/2 cup chopped nuts**

Pour into 9 x 5 x 3" loaf pan. Bake 350° for 1 hour or till toothpick comes out clean. Cool thoroughly before slicing. Wrap tightly in plastic wrap in packages of 4-6 slices each.

In the days of the Conquistadores, a teasponful of chia seeds was regarded as sufficient to sustain an Indian for a day on a forced march.

COTTAGE CHEESE-CHIA BREAD

Combine:

     1/4 cup margarine
     1/4 cup sugar
     2 eggs
     1 cup small-curd cottage cheese
     1/2 cup seedless raisins
     1/2 cup milk

Combine and add:

     2 cups flour
     4 tsp. baking powder
     1/4 tsp. soda
     1/4 tsp. salt
     1 tbls. chia seeds
     2 tbls. wheat germ

Stir in 1/4 cup hulled sunflower seeds.

Pour into greased and floured 8 x 8 x 2" square baking pan. Bake at 375° for 10 minutes. Reduce heat to 350° and bake about 40 minutes longer. Test with a toothpick.

Remove from pan and cool on a wire rack after 10 minutes cooling in the pan.

CRANBERRY-CHEESE LOAF

Sift together:
2 cups all-purpose flour
1 cup sugar
1-1/2 tsp. baking powder
1/2 tsp. soda
1/2 tsp. salt
2 tsp. fresh grated orange peel
Cut in: **2 tbls. shortening**

Squeeze the juice from one orange and add water to measure 3/4 cup. Add to the dry mixture.

Add: **1-1/2 cups shredded sharp cheddar cheese**
1 egg, beaten
1 cup chopped cranberries
1/2 cup finely chopped walnuts

Pour into loaf pan. Bake 350° for one hour or till a toothpick comes out clean. Remove from pan and cool on a wire rack. Chill in the refrigerator before slicing. Wrap slices in small packets for packing.

POPPY SEED BREAD

Combine:
1/4 cup margarine
1 cup sugar
2 eggs
1 tsp. grated fresh orange peel
Combine:
2 cups unsifted flour
2-1/2 tsp. baking powder
1/2 tsp. salt
1/4 tsp. nutmeg
Add alternately with **1 cup milk**
Fold in:
1/3 cup poppy seeds
1/2 cup chopped nuts
1/2 cup raisins

Pour into a greased and floured 9 x 5" loaf pan. Bake 350° for one hour or till a toothpick comes out clean. Cool in the pan 10 minutes before turning out to cool on a wire rack. Chill in the refrigerator before slicing.

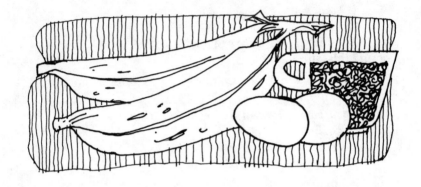

BANANA LOAF

Combine:
>   **1/2 cup shortening**
>   **1 cup sugar**

Add: **2 eggs**
>   **1 cup mashed ripe banana (2 medium)**
>   **1 tbls. lemon juice**

Combine and add:
>   **1 cup toasted wheat germ**
>   **2 cups flour**
>   **3 tsp. baking powder**
>   **1/2 tsp. salt**

Turn into greased loaf pan. Bake 350° for 50-60 minutes or till the center tests done with a toothpick. Cool in the pan 10 minutes. Turn out on a wire rack to cool. Chill before slicing.

HAWAIIN FRUIT LOAF

Combine:
>
> **1/2 cup margarine**
> **1 cup sugar**

Add: **2 eggs**
>
> **1/2 cup mashed ripe banana**

Combine and add:
>
> **2 cups flour**
> **1 tsp. baking powder**
> **1/2 tsp. baking soda**
> **1/2 tsp. salt**

Mix thoroughly:

Fold in:
>
> **1/2 cup crushed pineapple, undrained**
> **1/2 cup shredded coconut**

Pour into greased and floured 9 x 5″ loaf pan. Bake 350° for one hour and 10 minutes or till it tests done with a toothpick. Remove from the pan and cool on a wire rack. Chill in the refrigerator before slicing.

ANISE STICKS
(for licorice addicts)

This is particularly good with fruit and cheese.

Combine:
>
> **2 eggs**
> **2/3 cup sugar**
> **1 tsp. anise seed**
> **1 cup flour (unbleached, if available)**

This batter is very stiff.

Grease and flour a 9 x 5 x 3″ loaf pan. Spread the batter in the prepared pan. Bake 375° for 20-30 minutes or till a toothpick comes out clean. The pan will be less than half full. Remove the loaf from the pan and cut into 1/2″ slices with a sharp knife. Place slices on a lightly greased cookie sheet. Bake five minutes, or till bottoms of the slices are browned. Turn and bake five minutes more. Cool on a wire rack.

COCONUT TOAST

Combine:
> **1-1/2 cups milk**
> **1 egg**
> **1/2 tsp. vanilla**
> **1/4 tsp. almond extract**
> **1 cup toasted shredded coconut**

Combine and add:
> **3 cups flour**
> **3 tsp. baking powder**
> **1/2 tsp. salt**
> **1 cup sugar**

Pour into a greased 9 x 5 x 3" loaf pan. Bake at 350° about one hour and 10 minutes or till a toothpick comes out clean. Cool thoroughly before slicing. Use a sharp thin knife. Lay on oven racks to dry overnight, or till like Melba Toast. A gas pilot light should be enough to dry with. Use a 150-watt bulb in place of the oven light on an electric stove.

Butters and Spreads
NUT BREAD BUTTERS

Almond: Combine
> **1/2 cup softened margarine**
> **1 tbls. finely chopped almonds**
> **1/2 tsp. almond extract**

Date: Combine
> **1/2 cup softened margarine**
> **1/4 cup finely chopped dates**

Orange:
> **1/2 cup soft margarine**
> **1 tbls. orange juice**
> **1 tsp. grated orange rind**

Honey: **1/2 cup soft margarine**
> **2-3 tbls. honey**
> **Dash of cinnamon**

Honey-Orange:
> **1/2 cup soft margarine**
> **2 tbls. honey**
> **1 tsp. fresh grated orange peel**
> **Dash of nutmeg**

FRUIT-NUT SPREAD

In a covered saucepan, simmer:
> **1-1/2 cups lightly packed cut-up dry fruit**
> **(apricot, apple, prune, raisin, etc.)**
> **1 cup water**

Simmer 20-30 minutes or till soft and most of the water has evaporated. Place in a food blender with:
> **1/2 cup brown sugar, firmly packed**
> **1/2 tsp. cinnamon or nutmeg**

Whirl till smooth. Fold in 1/2 cup chopped almonds or walnuts. Use as a sandwich or cracker spread.

CHIA-CHEESE SPREAD
(This is high in protein and energy)

To a cheese spread like Kraft or Wispride add one of the following:

Chia seeds	Sesame seeds
Chopped walnuts	Sunflower seeds
Chopped dried apple	Pumpkin seeds
Poppy seeds	Caraway seeds

Spread on rye, pumpernickel or other whole-grain bread.

SURPRISE SANDWICH FILLINGS

For a hot sandwich, grill in a frying pan. Combine:
> Dried cottage cheese and strawberry jam. Add a drop of water
> if too dry. (See chapter on drying for cottage cheese.)
> Peanut butter and crumbled dried banana flakes or raisins.

Other sandwich suggestions:
> Cold cuts (chopped ham slices, salami, bologna, liverwurst)
> Bacon bar and chopped dried fruit combined
> Canned luncheon meats
> Cheeses, sliced or spreads
> Hard-cooked eggs
> Peanut butter and jelly or honey
> Canned tuna
> Canned chicken, ham, beef spreads. (Underwood brand)

Garnishes for the first day or two:
> Sliced cucumber
> Green pepper strips
> Tomato slices
> Onion slices
> Romaine lettuce
> Watercress
> Zucchini
> Carrot sticks cut very thin

TOASTED PUMPKIN OR SUNFLOWER SEEDS

Combine:

2 cups (14 oz.) seed, hulled
2 tbls. Worcestershire sauce or soy sauce
2 tbls. melted margarine
2 tbls. grated Parmesan or Romano cheese
Salt to taste (regular or garlic)

Mix all ingredients in a bowl, then spread out in a flat pan. Toast in a 375° oven, stirring every five minutes, for 15 minutes. Spread crackers or bread with peanut butter, cheese spread, or honey. Press upside down onto the toasted seeds for a nutritious addition. Toasted seeds are also good on ripe bananas and apple slices. Add to macaroni and cheese or scrambled eggs.

PITA BREAD

Pita bread is very practical for backpacking. When cut in half, a pita "loaf" forms two pockets to be stuffed with all sorts of fillings.
Interesting combinations can include:

Dry salami slices, Swiss cheese slices, Romaine lettuce leaf, carrot sticks.
Tuna, zucchini slices, chopped fresh parsley.
Peanut butter, jelly, celery sticks.

Pita bread can also be used as a "plate" if you have prepared a non-runny dinner combination.

5

Pepping Up Plain Water

. . . This cleft in the rock,
And white foaming waterfall;
Nature's wild stage set . . .

Water is absolutely essential to life, so liquids must form a large and important part of your outdoor diet. Sunshine, dry air, wind and perspiration all cause a loss of body moisture. If pollution is not a problem, sample every spring and creek that crosses your trail. You can be in real danger if you do not drink enough fluids. Take a salt tablet or two every few hours if you are perspiring heavily. Include water (and some food) at the same time.

Soups perform a very useful role when meal planning. Some may be enjoyed as appetizers—M B T packets, instant or cubed bouillon, Lipton Cup-O-Soup, Miso-shiru packets in the Oriental foods section. Other soups like Wyler's, Knorr, Golden Grain, Mrs. Grass, Top Ramen, Maggi and Lipton are more hearty. The addition of dried vegetables and meats with instant rice, no-cook noodles (Mrs. Reis Egg Noodles) or Oriental alimentary paste will provide a quick and tasty one-pot meal. Look for the soups that take only 5-10 minutes to cook.

Late in the day, when the temperature is dropping and you are tired from a long day, a cup of soup can be very satisfying. Fatigue is often a symptom of dehydration. A hot drink will introduce liquids back into your body.

Soup Variations and Combinations

- Blend a few ounces of shredded cheese (cheddar, Jack, Swiss) with hot soups for flavor and protein.
- Add crumbled dried leaves from spinach, kale, Romaine lettuce, chard, or dried zucchini slices. (See chapter on drying.)
- Add instant potato flakes to thicken soups.
- Add dry milk and coffee lightener to make a "creamed" soup.

Combine:

> Wyler's Potato with Leek and Chicken Soup.
> Vegetable soup and beef noodle soup.
> Minestrone and onion soup with a sprinkle of Parmesan cheese.
> Pea soup with dry milk, dry parsley, celery leaves and onion.
> Beef or checken noodle soup plus dried vegetables, mushrooms.
> Tomato soup plus dried tuna or dried shrimp (See chapter on drying.)

A "cozy" made from toweling to fit your cooking pot will keep the foods you are rehydrating warm. One made for your coffee pot will keep soup, coffee, or tea warm.

Coffees

Two ways to carry pre-measured individual servings:

1—Use a long, narrow plastic bag. Measure individual portions. Place one measure in the bottom of the bag, tie a string around the top with a bow knot, add another portion, tie another string. Continue to top of bag and tie off.

2—Measure individual pre-mixed servings, fold into doubled foil squares. Corral the packets in a plastic bag.

SPICED COFFEE

In a saucepan, heat to boiling:

2 cups water
1 tbls. brown sugar
2-3 cinnamon sticks
1 tsp. grated orange peel
1/4 tsp. whole allspice

Strain while pouring into cups containing 1 tsp. instant coffee powder.

European coffee or hot chocolate mixes divided into individual portions in a narrow plastic bag.

VANILLA MOCHA MIX

Combine in a large bowl:

1 cup cocoa
2 cups sugar
2 cups dry milk
2 cups dry coffee lightener
1/2 cup instant coffee

Divide and pack into four jars and include 1/4 of a vanilla bean in each jar. (Available in spice section.) Seal with a tight lid and store in the refrigerator a week before using, to allow the mix to absorb the vanilla flavor from the bean. To serve: Allow approximately 3 level tbls. of mix for each serving.

6-1/2 cups dry mix

MOCHA COFFEE

For each serving combine:

1 tsp. instant coffee
1 tbls. cocoa
1 tsp. powdered sugar

Variations: Substitute a square or two from a chocolate bar for the cocoa. Use carob powder instead of chocolate. (Health food store.)

At camp: add hot water.

IRISH COFFEE

At home, combine thoroughly in a plastic bag:
   1/2 cup coffee lightener (Preem, Coffee Mate)
   1/4 cup powdered sugar
   6 tbls. granulated sugar
   4 heaping tsp. instant coffee

At camp: Heat 3 cups water to boiling and add dry ingredients. Put 2 tbls. whiskey (1 oz.) into each cup. Add hot coffee mixture.
4 servings

CONTINENTAL COFFEE MIX

Combine thoroughly:
   2/3 cup instant coffee powder
   1 cup hot chocolate mix
   1 cup coffee lightener
   1/2 cup sugar
   1/2 tsp. cinnamon (optional)

At camp: Use 3-4 heaping teaspoons per cup. Add hot water and stir till mixed well. Top with a dollop of margarine.

EUROPEAN COFFEE FLAVORS

For each cup, start with:

1 rounded tsp. instant coffee
2 heaping tsp. hot chocolate mix

Flavor with one of the following:

1/4 tsp. cinnamon
1/4 tsp. nutmeg
1 drop almond extract
1 drop vanilla extract
1 drop mint extract
4-6 pastel party mints
1/2 tsp. brown sugar
1/2 tsp. white sugar
1/2 tsp. powdered sugar

For more "body" add dry milk or coffee lightener. Top with a teaspoonful of margarine.

TEA TIPS

An enamel pot will brew clearer tea than an aluminum one. Though tea bags are handy to use, they often contain the "sweepings" and tea dust. Horniman's, Bigelow and Red Rose are among the exceptions.

Consider buying loose tea such as Ty-phoo black tea, or try a specialty shop dealing in tea blends. You get more tea flavor from less weight.

Spiced Constant Comment Tea comes bagged or loose, and is a nice tea with sweets and desserts.

Herb teas and Oriental teas are distinctive. Try several kinds to choose your favorites.

TEA FLAVORINGS

To hot tea, add your choice:

        Whole cloves [or a dash of ground cloves)
        Dry orange peel
        Orange marmalade
        Clear fruit jellies (grape, mint, apple)
        Flavored gelatin (cherry is delicious)
        Crushed peppermint candy stick
        6-8 pastel after-dinner mints
        Honey
        Citrus crystals (Start, Tang)
        Packaged lemonade mix
        Brown or white sugar

SPICED TEA MIX

Use two heaping teaspoons per cup. Combine thoroughly:

    1 cup instant tea
    1 cup citrus crystals (Start, Tang)
    1 pkg. lemonade mix
    1/2 cup powdered sugar
    1 tsp. cinnamon
    1/2 tsp. ground cloves

Add hot water after measuring dry mix into cup.

Citrus crystals (Start, Tang, lemonade mixes) are refreshing and delicious when dissolved in hot water. They all taste especially good when you are tired. Wyler's and Kool-Aid both have lemonade mix complete with sugar in bulk cans (1 lb. 8 oz.). Measure what you will need into a Ziploc bag, or individual packets.

Chocolate

Cocoa products contain theobromine, which mildly stimulates the mental processes and the muscular system.

HOT COCOA

At home, combine:

1/3 cup sugar
1/3 cup cocoa
1/4 tsp. salt
1-1/2 cups dry milk
1/2 cup coffee lightener (Preem, Coffee-Mate)

At camp: Place dry contents in cooking pot. Add about 1/4 cup cold water and mix till all ingredients are wet. Add 5-1/2 cups water, stirring continually. Heat to a simmer. DO NOT BOIL.

Variations: Top each serving with several miniature marshmallows. Add a dash of cinnamon. Add a tsp. of instant coffee per cup.

7-8 servings

CHOCOLATE MALTED

For each serving, combine:

2 heaping tsp. hot chocolate mix
1 tbls. malted milk powder
1/3 cup dry milk
1 tsp. coffee lightener (optional)

At camp: add 1 cup cold stream water and stir vigorously. Clean snow can be added if available.

Flavorful Drinks

CHIA

Chia seeds (health food store) are known to the Indians of the Southwest as "concentrated energy." As noted, one tablespoon of chia seeds was used to sustain themselves for 24 hours on a hard march.

HONEY-CHIA DRINK

In a cup place:
>**1 tsp. chia seeds**
>**1 tsp. citrus crystals**
>**Honey to taste**

Fill the cup half full of hot water. Let set five minutes, then add more hot water.

Add 1 tsp. chia seeds to cereals, soups, pancake mix, or omelet.

ORANGE NOG

At home, combine:
>**1 cup dry milk**
>**1/4 cup coffee lightener**
>**1 tbls. sugar**
>**1/3 cup orange juice crystals (Tang, Start)**

At camp: Add 3 cups cold water and stir vigorously.

Variations: Use Tang grape crystals instead of orange. Use flavored gelatin. To with a sprig of wild mint.

3-4 servings

EGGNOG

For each serving, combine:
>   **2 tbls. dry egg powder**
>   **1 tbls. brown sugar**
>   **Dash of salt**
>   **1/3 cup dry milk**
>   **1/4 cup coffee lightener**
>   **Dash of cinnamon or nutmeg**

Be sure the dry ingredients are well mixed.

At camp: Add 1 cup cold water and blend with a wire whip or fork.

CRANBERRY MULL

At home, combine and tie in a cheesecloth bag:
>   **1 tbls. whole cloves, 1 tsp. allspice (whole), and one**
>   **six-inch cinnamon stick, broken**

In a plastic bag, combine:
>   **1/4 cup sugar, 1/4 tsp. salt, 1/2 cup grapefruit drink**
>   **crystals (Tang)**

Also include **1/2 cup dry crushed cranberries** (see chapter on drying).

At camp: Heat 4-5 cups water. Add dry cranberry powder and simmer till rehydrated. Add the rest of the ingredients and simmer, covered, five minutes. Remove spice bag and serve.

5-6 servings

BANANA MILK SHAKE

For each serving: combine
>   **1/3 cup dry milk**
>   **1/4 cup coffee lightener**
>   **2 tbls. crushed dry banana flakes**

At camp: Add one cup cold water and stir or shake vigorously.

Variation: Add an instant chocolate drink packet.

FRUITY SHAKE

At home, combine: **Contents of one package of pre-sweetened fruit drink (Kool-Aid, Wyler's)**
1 cup dry milk
1/4 cup coffee lightener

At camp: Fill a quart plastic bottle half full of water. Add dry mix and shake vigorously. Add water to about an inch from the top and shake again.

FLAVORED BUTTERMILK

Combine:
6 tbls. dry buttermilk powder (Darigold brand)
2 tbls. coffee lightener
2 tbls. brown sugar
2 tbls. orange juice crystals

Add 1-1/2 cups cold water, stirring till smooth.

2 servings

COFFEE LIGHTENER EQUIVALENTS
(Preem, Coffee-Mate, Cremora)

Water	Lightener	Equivalent
1 cup	1/4 cup	1 cup milk
1 cup	1/2 cup	1 cup light cream
1 cup	3/4 cup	1 cup heavy cream

6

Be Your Own Supermarket Gourmet:

Planning meals with brand name foods from the market shelf

. . . An overcast day.
An overturned pot of soup.
An overlooked book . . .

When searching the supermarket for trail foods, pay close attention to the contents of packaged mixes. You often can closely duplicate the ingredients for less money. For instance: McCormick and Co. puts out "Skillet Magic." A 5-3/8 oz. package consists of 2 cups broken narrow noodles and about 2 tbls. of concentrated flavoring. This includes instant beef bouillon, dry garlic, dry celery, dry onion, salt and a little cornstarch for thickening, plus preservatives. It is up to you to add the fresh hamburger.

If you buy packaged noodles, mix a flavoring of 1 tbls. instant bouillon, and pinches of the other seasonings to make up the second tablespoon, then add a tsp. of cornstarch if you wish to, you have duplicated their package. Now add textured vegetable protein (t.v.p.) or your own cooked dried meat and some dry vegetables for a complete one-pot meal.

Washington's Center for Science in the Public Interest says, "The most nutritious snacks you can eat are granola and milk, almonds, peanuts, cashew nuts and peaches." Excellent sources of protein include canned salmon, tuna, sardines, clams, oysters, corned beef and Vienna sausages. All these foods make good trail nutrition.

A backpacker friend who recently completed the entire 2,500 miles of the Pacific Crest Trail recommends "Same Thing . . . start with a pasta (spaghetti, noodles, macaroni), add tuna or any seafood, and real cheddar cheese (not powdered). To spice things up add dried celery and onion flakes, salt and pepper, and lots of powdered milk."

He also says, "One good snack food that can be thrown together right outside the store is: equal parts honey, peanut butter and oatmeal or granola. Vary it with raisins or chopped dates. Really a tasty concoction!"

Dumplings make a good "stick-to-the-ribs" addition to soups and stews. They can be made from Bisquick or corn muffin mix according to package directions. A stiff batter made from cream of wheat, dry milk, salt and a little water can be cooked briefly and individually on a spoon in the simmering liquid before scooping it off to float on its own. This will help to keep the batter "glued" together while cooking. Fruit compotes can be enhanced with cake mix or brownie mix "dumplings." Add ginger bread mix dumplings to hot applesauce.

Parkay liquid margarine seems to go further, tends to burn less easily, comes in a reasonably safe container, and will keep up to a week unrefrigerated if care is taken to keep it in the inner recesses of your pack out of the sun. Chilling each night in a cold stream will help, too. Use it in place of cooking oil, to spread on bread, and add to casseroles and soups for better flavor.

Search specialty food stores for interesting lightweight foods. Japanese and Jewish stores have soup cubes. Italians love their hard dry salamis and cheeses. If you can't find it in your own market, Greek shops have pita (pocket) bread. Cut open, then stuff with a non-runny casserole or scrambled eggs. No plate to wash!

Rice is a good basic food for breakfast or dinner combinations. Try adding scrambled eggs and onion, cheddar cheese, dry parsley and celery leaves, toasted almonds, grated dried orange or lemon rind, citrus pulp dried, clear jellies or marmalade, dried vegetables and meat rehydrated, bouillon or packaged soups, t.v.p., stewed dried fruits. Plan three or four package-suggested servings of instant rice for two hungry hikers.

Packaged dry soup mixes can be thickened by adding your own

dry vegetables and meat or fish, textured vegetable protein or pastas such as small-sized macaroni or noodles. Instant mashed potato will also give a soup more body. Look in the Oriental section for packages of alimentary paste that looks like white spaghetti or squiggly noodles. These usually take only three minutes to cook. Break it up as you add it to the hot liquid to make it easier to eat.

Granolas with NO preservatives can be purchased when on sale and stored sealed in a plastic bag in the freezer for future use. Granola bars are equally tasty for breakfast, lunch, or a before-bed snack.

The following ideas suggest ways you can use convenience foods:

Golden Grain or Kraft Macaroni and Cheese—Add rehydrated beef or chicken (see chapter on drying), dry salami slices, dried tomato paste leather, tomato slices that have been dried, or dry parsley, celery, or onion flakes.

Betty Crocker Tuna Helper—Prepare by the skillet method, using dried and rehydrated tuna or shrimp (see chapter on drying). You can also add onion flakes, sliced celery, green pepper cubes, sliced mushrooms, corn, or peas.

Lipton's Mushroom Cup-O-Soup—To two cups boiling water add two pkgs. soup, 3/4 cup instant rice, 1/2 tsp. rosemary, 1/2 small jar of chipped beef, 1/2 cup dried frozen peas. Simmer 7-10 minutes. Serves 2.

Top Ramen Stew—Serves 3-4. To four cups boiling water, add one cup dried mixed vegetables (peas, carrots, chard, celery slices, etc.) one tbls. dry onion flakes, 1/4 cup broken dried mushroom pieces, 1/4 cup chopped dry salami. Cover and remove from heat for 10 minutes to rehydrate dry vegetables. Return to a boil. Add Ramen noodles. Cook 3-5 minutes. Add soup packet and simmer 2-3 minutes more.

Curried Ramen Soup—Measure 4-1/2 cups cold water. Add one oz. (about 1/3 cup) dry mushroom slices. Rehydrate 10-15 minutes. Remove mushrooms and set aside in individual soup bowls or cups. Bring the water to a boil. Add one tbls. curry powder and two pkgs. broken Ramen soup noodles. Boil for three minutes, stirring once or twice. Add soup packets. Simmer 2-3 minutes more. Serve over the rehydrated mushrooms. Serves 3-4.

Potato Casseroles—Add dried cooked meats and dried rehydrated vegetables. Prepare according to skillet directions.

Hash Brown Potatoes—Combine with dried or canned and drained tuna or shrimp for a satisfying main meal. (Rinse the shrimp before using.)

Albers Quick Grits—Make the grits with instant bouillon and top with a gravy mix to which you have added rehydrated meat and vegetable.

SUPERMARKET SHOPPING LIST
KITCHEN AIDS

Squeeze Parkey (liquid margarine)—Kraft Foods, Chicago, Ill. 60690
Convenient for cooking and spreading.

Pan Pal Solid (pan coating)—Pan Pal, North Hollywood, Cal 91605
Prevents sticking

(A rubber spatula comes in handy for clean-up, especially at a dry camp.)

Ziploc Storage Bags, 7 x 8, 10 x 11"—Dow Chemical Co., Indianapolis, Ind. 46268. Packaging dry mixes, leakproof, durable.

Teri Nylon reinforced towles—Kimberly Clark Corp. Neenah, Wis. 54956
Disposable dishtowels and wash cloths

Tuf 'N Ready Towels—Crown-Zellerbach Corp., San Francisco, Cal. 94119
Disposable dishtowels and wash cloths

Handi-Wipes—Colgate-Palmolive Co., New York 10022
Reusable rayon cloth. Dries quickly

Wonder Cloths—Personal Products Co., Milltown, N.J. 08850
Reusable rayon cloth. Dries quickly.

Wash 'N Dri Towelettes—Canaan Products, Inc., Canaan, Conn. 08850
Emergency clean-up. Disposable.

Keen Scour Cloths (three in pack)—Kurly Kate, Chicago, Ill. 60616
Lightweight pot scratcher

Dixie Bowls (6" size) — American Can Co., Greenwich, Conn. 06830
Plastic coated for waterless camps

Heavyweight plastic cutlery — Forster Mfg. Co., Wilton, Maine 04294
Lightweight spoons, knives, forks

Kirk's Coco Hardwater Castile — Procter and Gamble, Cincinnati, Ohio
45202. Bar soap

Fel's Naptha Soap — Purex Corp., Lakewood, Calif. 90712
Bar soap good for poison ivy and oak

SEASONINGS

Bits 'O Bacon — Wilson and Co., Oklahoma City, Okla. 73105
100% real bacon. Add to eggs, soups, sandwiches, vegetables

Bac-O's — Betty Crocker, Minneapolis, Minn. 55460
Imitation bacon (t.v.p.)

Imitation Bacon Bits — Schilling, Inc., Baltimore, Md. 21202
1 tbls. = 1 slice crisp bacon

Seasoned croutons — French's, Rochester, N.Y. 14609
Soup or casserole topping, fondue

Dry flakes of onion, garlic, parsley, celery, green peppers, etc.

Cinnamon Sugar — Schilling, Baltimore, Md. 21202
Toast, applesauce, hot cereal, pancakes

Sauce mixes for — chili, tacos, spaghetti, sloppy joes, sour cream, stroganoff, Spanish rice, cheese, wine sauces

Gravy mixes — check cooking time for all mixes. Use them for rice
topping or thickening and flavoring for stews

BREAKFAST BARS

Food Sticks — Pillsbury Co., Minneapolis, Minn. 55402
Chocolate, peanut butter

Breakfast Bar — Carnation Co.
6 bars to pkg: chocolate, cinnamon, peanut butter

Breakfast Squares — General Mills
8 bars: chocolate, vanilla, cinnamon or butter pecan

Granola Bars — Nature Valley
12 bars: cinnamon, coconut

Crunchola — Sunfield Foods, St. Louis, Mo. 63127
8 bars: peanut butter

Pop Tarts — Kellogg's
10 flavors

Wholemeal Biscuits — Crawford's (imported from Great Britain)
Milk chocolate. High nutrition.

Tiger's Milk Protein Cookies — Tiger's Milk Products, Irvine, Cal. 92705
Diet food section. High in vitamins and minerals

DRY CEREALS

Granolas—Quaker, Nature Valley, Country Morning
  Breakfast—hot or cold
100% Bran—Nabisco Co.
  High fiber cereal
Bran Buds—Kellogg Company
  High fiber cereal
Concentrate—Kellogg Co.
  High quality protein. Add to casseroles and meats, also
Grape Nuts—Post (General Foods)
  Good hot or cold, or added to other cereals
Uncle Sam Cereal—Uncle Sam Breakfast Food Co., Omaha, Neb. 68111
  Natural laxative. (Flax seeds)
Bircher Muesli Cereal—Reese Finer Foods, Chicago, Ill. 60614
  Breakfast, fruit topping

COOKED CEREALS

Roman Meal-Instant or 5-minute—Roman Meal Co., Tacoma, Wash.
  98409. Whole grain cereal
Maypo—30-second—Malt-O-Meal Co., Minneapolis, Minn. 55402
  Wheat
Malt-O-Meal—1-minute—Malt-O-Meal Co., Minneapolis, Minn. 55402.
  Wheat
Wheatena—5-minute—Standard Milling
  Wheat germ/bran
Ralston—Instant—Ralston Purina Co., St. Louis, Mo. 63188
  Whole wheat
Wheat Hearts—3-5 minute—General Mills
  Whole wheat
Quaker Hot and Creamy—2-1/2-minute—Quaker Oats Company
  Wheat
Quaker Whole Wheat—1-minute—Quaker Oats Company
  Wheat

Cream of Rice — 30-second — Grocery Store Products, West Chester, Pa.
Rice

Cream of Wheat — Regular, quick, instant, mix 'n eat — Nabisco Co.
Enriched farina

Instant Quaker Oatmeal — various flavors in individual packs — Quaker
Oats Company. Make-in-a-bowl oatmeal

Old Fashioned and Quick Quaker Oats — Quaker Oats Co.
Regular oatmeal

Albers Grits and Albers Corn Meal
"Mush"

PANCAKES

Complete pancake mixes — Betty Crocker, Aunt Jemima, Cinch, Martha
White Flapstax Buttermilk. Just add water

Corn bread and muffin mix — Cinch, Jiffy, Dromedary (Nabisco)
Add more liquid for corn pancakes

Bisquick — Betty Crocker (General Mills)
Pancakes, dumplings

OTHER MIXES

Hash Browns with Onions — Betty Crocker
Add to a soup mix for a chowder

Scrambled Egg Mix and Western Omelette Mix — Durkee
Good for a change

MUNCH AND LUNCH

**Canned liverwurst, chicken spread, corned beef, roast beef, deviled
ham** — Wm. Underwood, Westwood, Mass. 02090. Canned meat
spreads for lunches and to mix with eggs

Pepperoni Pepkins — Swift and Co., Chicago, Ill. 60604
Similar to dry salami

Dry Salami — Gallo, San Francisco, Calif. 94107
Continues to dry and harden if left out

Condensed mince meat and NoneSuch Mince meat — Borden, Inc.,
Columbus, Ohio 43215. Trail snack, or whirl in blender for fruit leather

Peanut Butter — Your choice. Transfer to a plastic container

Spun or whipped honey — Easy to spread. Less drip and mess

Canned brown breads — Remove from can and slice. Wrap tightly in
plastic wrap or foil for trail

Party Pumpernickel Bread — Cocktail size loaf. Use for lunch or dinner.
Made of unbleached white and rye flour

**English muffins, bread sticks, pita (pocket) bread, French or French
sourdough breads** — all keep well

CHEESE

Velveeta and American—Kraft Foods, Chicago, Ill. 60690
  Not refrigerated. Sticky. Velveeta has less calories and fat
Cheez Whiz (in a jar)—Kraft Foods, Chicago, Ill. 60690
  Cracker spread, vegetable sauce, added to scrambled eggs
Cheez Kisses—Borden, Inc.
  Individually wrapped, high protein snacks
Swiss Castle cheese triangles—Imported from Switzerland
  Snacks or lunch, individually wrapped
Squeez-A-Snack—Kraft
  Various flavors, no waste, plastic wrapped
Kraft Cracker Barrel cheese—wrapped, mellow, sharp, extra sharp
  Good for snacks or for cooking
Kraft Cold Pack cheese food—Various flavors. Cheese spread
Tillamook Hard Cheeses—Various flavors. Good cooking cheeses
Fintinella, Provolone, Kasseri, Edam, Guda, Jack, Cheddar and Gruyere
  —wrapped in small wedges all travel well. Keep in a plastic bag or wrap
  in plastic wrap or foil to keep the oil contained
Grated Parmesan or Parmesan/Romano cheese—Needs no refrigeration.
  Sprinkle on hot breads, soup, popcorn

CRACKERS

Roman Meal Wafers—American Biscuit Co., Battle Creek, Mich. 49016
  Lunch cracker
Holland Rusk Instant Toast—Nabisco Import
  French toast, open sandwich
Devonsheer Melba Toast—Devonsheer Melba Corp., Carlstadt, N.J.
  07072. Plain, rye, wheat
Ryvita Rye Bread—Ryvita Co., Poole, Dorset, England
  Lunch snacks
Ry Krisp Whole Grain Crackers—Ralston Purina Co., St. Louis, Mo.
  63188. Seasoned and plain
Hardtack Crisp Rye Bread—Zinsmaster Co., Minneapolis, Minn. 55440
  Scored to break into wafers
Sailor Boy Pilot Breas—American Biscuit Co., Tacoma, Wash. 98409
  Enriched wheat flour crackers
Roman Meal, Stoned Wheat, Sesame Crisp Wafers—American Biscuit Co.
  Wholesome lunch crackers
Wheat Thins, Ritz, Triscuit—Nabisco Co., East Hanover, N.J. 07936
  Lunch crackers
Waverly Wafers—Nabisco Company
  Three wrapped packets to box
Cinnamon Treats—Nabisco Company
  Graham crackers in packets

DRIED FRUITS

Dates, figs, prunes, apricots, apples, mixed fruits, raisins — use as is, make into fruit logs, stew

Dromedary pitted dates — Nabisco, Inc., N.Y. 10022
Lighter weight when pitted

Fruit Roll — A Sahadi Co., Moonachie, N.J. 07074
Fruit leathers

Apple Snack — Weight Watchers, Manhasset, N.Y. 11030
1/2 oz. = 1 medium apple

CANDY

Miniature Bars (Individually wrapped) — Nestle Co., White Plains, N.Y. 10605. Add to gorp bag

Semi-Sweet Chocolate Morsels — Nestle Co., White Plains, N.Y. 10605. Add to gorp bag.

Butterscotch Bits — Nestle Co., White Plains, N.Y. 10606
Add to gorp bag

M and M's (peanut or plain) — Mars, Inc., Hackettstown, N.J. 07840
Gorp mix

Cadbury Milk Chocolate — Cadbury Corp., Stamford, Conn. 06905
Creamy, various flavors

Hard Candies — Jelly beans, sour and butter balls, lemon drops, peppermints, licorice, butterscotch discs, etc.

NUTS AND ASSORTED GORP

Peanuts, mixed nuts, cashews, pecans, almonds

Fisher's Sunflower Nuts (toasted and salted) — Use for snacks, and topping for crackers and peanut butter, honey, etc.

Nuts and seeds in the shell — Salted sunflower seeds, pistachios, calabaza, toasted corn kernels, etc.

Hawaiian Holiday Coconut Chips — Hawaiian Holiday, Inc., Honokaa, Hawaii 96727. Snacks

Hawaiian Macadamia Nuts — Hawaiian Holiday, Inc., Honokaa, Hawaii 96727. Snacks

Coconut — Angel Flake or Shredded

Frenchies Shoe String Potatoes and Pringles Potato Chips — in a can for added salt.

LIQUIDS

Breakfast Drink Crystals — Borden's Orange Flavor Breakfast Drink, Tang Orange, Grape, Grapefruit flavors (General Foods), Start Orange Flavored Drink (General Foods)

Dry Milk (non-fat) — Carnation, various house brands, etc.
For cooking and drinking

Dry Milk (low-fat) — Milkman by Foremost
Make a paste first before adding all the water

Coffee Mate non-dairy creamer — Carnation Co., Los Angeles, Calif.
90036. Improves flavor of dry milk

Cremora non-dairy creamer — Borden, Inc., Columbus, Ohio 43215
Improves flavor of dry milk

Preem non-dairy creamer — Early California Ind. Inc., Los Angeles, Calif
Improves flavor of dry milk

Drinking Gelatin, plain or orange — Knox Gelatin, Inc., Englewood Cliffs,
N.J.. 78% MDR, protein; 45% MDR, Vit. C per 1-oz. serving

P D Q Milk Flavoring (chocolate) — Ovaltine Products, Villa Park, Ill.
60181. Add to milk or dessert topping

Hot Cocoa Mixes (individual packets) — Carnation, Nestle, Swiss
Miss, Ovaltine, Hershey's

Instant Malted Milk — Carnation Co., Los Angeles, Calif. 90036
Add to milk

Ovaltine (Malt and chocolate) — Ovaltine Products
Hot or cold drink

Instant Coffee — Various manufacturers
Hot or cold drink

European Style Coffees — Hills Bros., General Foods
Flavored coffees

Full Bodied Teas — Lyons English, Hornimans English, Bigelow
Loose and bags. Strong. Takes less

Wyler's Drink Mixes — Borden Inc., Northbrook, Ill. 60062
Good hot or cold. Sugar added

Kool-Aid Drink Mixes — General Foods Corp., White Plains, N.Y. 10625
Good hot or cold. Sugar added

Lipton Tea Mixes, Nestea Tea Mixes — Good hot or cold

Rock Candy (pure cane sugar) — Dryden and Palmer, Long Island City,
N.Y. 11101. Sweetener for hot drinks

Romanoff M B T Broth packets — Riviana Foods, Houston, Texas 77001
Hot drink, seasoning, add to t.v.p. for flavoring

Steero Bouillon — American Kitchen Products, Jersey City, N.J. 07303
Cubes and instant. Drink or base for one-pot meal

Herb-Ox Instant Broth packets — The Pure Food Co., Mamaroneck,
N.Y. 10543. Onion, beef, chicken

Maggi Instant Broth packets — Nestle Co., White Plains, N.Y. 10605
Vegetable, beef, chicken

Maruchan's Wonton Soup Mix — Maruchan Inc., Box 30207, Los
Angeles, Calif. 90030. Cooks in three minutes

Rieber and Sons — Norway import — shrimp, crab, lobster soup mix
Add milk, Cooks in five minutes

Lipton Cup-a-Soup (Instant) — Thomas Lipton, Inc., Englewood Cliffs,
N.J. 07632. Drink, sauce, base for one-pot meal

Lipton Soup Packets — Thomas Lipton, Inc., Englewood Cliffs, N.J.
07632. Cooking required

Knorr Soups — Imported from Switzerland. Cooking required

Maggi Soup Mixes — Imported from Switzerland. Cooking required

Wyler's Soup Mixes — Borden Foods, Chicago, Ill. 60618
Cooking required

Mrs. Grass Soup Mixes — Hygrade Food Products, Bellwood, Ill. 60104
Cooking required

FROZEN AND CANNED FOODS TO DRY

Fruit Fresh (ascorbic acid mix) — Calgon Consumer Products, Pittsburgh, Pa. 15230. For keeping color and flavor in fruits and vegetables to be dried

Frozen fruits — strawberries, cherries, raspberries, cranberries
Dry as "leather" or whole for snacks

Frozen Vegetables — (DO NOT use any prepared with sauces.) Corn,
peas, cauliflower, spinach, green beans, (cut, not French), asparagus,
broccoli, zucchini, carrots, lima beans. Birdseye has "5-minute" vegetables. These will take less time to cook at camp

Sliced canned pineapple will dry sweeter than fresh. Add banana or
apple to crushed pineapple for leather

Frozen Tiny Alaska Shrimp — Del Monte Foods, Clinton, Iowa 52734
Fully cooked and cleaned. Dry as is

Kitchen Ready Frozen Shrimp — Carnation, Los Angeles, Calif. 90024
Fully cooked and cleaned. Dry as is

Canned water-packed shrimp and tuna — Carnation, Starkist, Chicken of
the Sea. Drain well and dry

Ham — canned and fully cooked, ham steaks in deli, pieces of ham trimmings. Trim all fat before drying. Very salty, use sparingly

CANNED MEATS

Important—Refrigeration not necessary till opened. Buy the size needed
for one meal, with left-overs for breakfast

Dak Chopped Pork (1 lb.)—Danish Import
Good for two servings each dinner and breakfast

Plumrose Cooked Ham (1 lb.)—Danish Import
Good for two servings each dinner and breakfast

Vienna sausages, sliced dried beef, boned chicken—various companies

PROTEIN, PASTAS, DUMPLINGS

Textured Vegetable Protein (T.V.P.)—is made of soy beans. It can
be added to soups, hamburger "helper" mixes

Granburger—Worthington Foods, Inc. Comes in a waxed milk carton
container. Soak in hot water 3-5 minutes

Burger Savor—Armour, Inc., Phoenix, Ariz. 85077
Flavored mixes with seasonings and bread crumbs added

Proteinettes—Creamette Co., Minneapolis, Minn. 55401
Beef and ham flavors. Needs boiling and can be included when
boiling macaroni, etc. Add to omelets, cheese sauce, scalloped
potato mix

Mrs. Filbert's Plus Meat—J.H. Filbert, Inc., Baltimore, Md. 21229
Soak 5 minutes before adding to other ingredients

Fritini Vegetable Patties—Richter Bros., Inc., Carlstadt, N.J. 07072
Use with eggs, cheese, tomato dishes

Dried lentils—Blackeye peas, beans including limas, black, red, kidney,
pinto, white, garbanzo. All can be cooked and dried at home to
save on fuel and time at camp

Minute Rice—General Foods Corp., White Plains, N.Y. 10625
Quick and easy base for breakfast or dinner

Uncle Ben's Quick Rice—Uncle Ben's Foods, Houston, Texas 77001
Cooks in five minutes

Mrs. Reis Egg Noodles—Reis Noodle Co., North Hollywood, Calif.
91605. No cooking. Add to boiling water and soak three minutes

Pastas—Curlies, salad macaroni, shells, elbow macaroni, spaghetti,
noodles, etc.

Maggi Spaetzle—Maggi Company, Switzerland
Tiny dumplings added to soups, or use in place of macaroni. Cooks
in 15 minutes

Baking Mixes—Corn Bread Mixes-Cinch, Jiffy, Dromedary
Pancakes, hush puppies, dumplings, biscuits

Bisquick—General Mills
Pancakes, dumplings

Nabisco Spoon Size Shredded Wheat—Nabisco, Inc., East Hanover,
Crush and use as base for gravy combos

Nabisco Shredded Wheat—Nabisco, Inc., East Hanover,
Crush and use as base for gravy combos

CASSEROLES

Globe A-1—One-pot dinner complete with soy protein

Betty Crocker Potato Casseroles—General Mills, Minneapolis, Minn. 55460. Can be cooked in fry pan if watched carefully

French's Potato Casseroles—French, Rochester, N.Y. 14609
Use the potatoes to add to your own combinations. Check the cooking times

Betty Crocker Hash Browns/Onions—General Mills
Breakfast or dinner entree

Frenchies Potato Stix—Bell Brand Foods, Los Angeles, Calif. 90051
Snack or base for hot meal combo

French Fried Onion Rings—Durkee Foods, Cleveland, Ohio 44115
Add to casseroles, skillet meals

Instant potatoes—Can be used to thicken soups, coat fish for frying, add to clam chowder, make potato pancakes

Rice-A-Roni (Chicken, Beef, Spanish)—Golden Grain Co., San Leandro, Calif. Add meat and vegetable for complete meal

Various Noodles Romanoff, lasagna, etc.—Add vegetables, meat, t.v.p.

Kraft Dinners—Kraft Foods, Chicago, Ill. 60690
Add vegetables, meat, t.v.p.

Hamburger Helper, Tuna Helper—Betty Crocker
Add dried ground beef, tuna, t.v.p.

Make A Better Burger—Lipton
Flavored t.v.p.

DESSERTS

Bread, muffin, cake mixes—can be used to fry cookies at camp if less liquid is used. Make a stiff batter

Chocolate Chip Cookie Mix—Nestle Co., White Plains, N.Y. 10605
Add one egg and water. Cook in fry pan

Frosting Mixes—Any brand. Make candy according to package directions

Flavored gelatins, instant puddings, canned puddings, shortbreads, cookies, graham crackers

HEALTH FOODS

Fritini Vegetable Burger Mix—Swiss Import
High protein content.

Seelect Herb Teas—Seelect Products, Huntington Park, Calif. 90225
Natural herb teas

El Molino Natural Grains—El Molino Mills, City of Industry, Calif. 91746
Bran, oats, soya, raw wheat germ, etc.

Pernuts Soy Nuts—Flavor Tree Foods, Franklin Park, Ill. 60131
Sea salted snack

Fearn Soy-O Pancake Mix—Fearn Soya Foods, Melrose Park, Ill. 60160
Whole wheat and soya flour

Banana Chips, Trail Snack—AuNaturelle, Los Angeles, Calif. 90021
  Snakcs

Seeds, including sunflower, pumpkin, sesame, chia, etc.—For additions
  to casseroles, snacks, pancakes, pre-baked breads

Wheat Germ (Kretschmer Toasted)—International Multifoods, Minneapolis, Minn. 55402. Add to cereals, breads, milk, meat, fruit and
  vegetable topping.

(Sunflower seeds can be purchased from a pet shop for a lot less money.
  Toast your own in a hot fry pan.)

GOURMET SECTION

Mussels in red sauce, smoked frog legs, smoked octupus, clams, oysters
  —Reese Finer Foods, New York, Los Angeles, Chicago

Baby lobsters, fried grasshoppers and ants.

Diamondback Rattlesnake—Sue Ann Food Products, Chicago, Ill.

Baby Corn On Cob—Reese Finer Foods
  Can be drained and dried

Reese Lemony Lemon—Reese Finer Foods
  Instant lemon powder for drinks and sprinkling on salad vegetables

**Yorkshire Pudding Mix, Hollandaise Sauce Mix, Canned Date and
  Nut Loaf**

JEWISH FOODS

Instant soup or seasoning—Carmel Kosher Food Products, Chicago, Ill.
  Onion, chicken, mushroom mixes

Soup Nuts—Manischewitz, Newark, N.J., and Aron Streit, N.Y.
  Add to soups and stews

Potato Pancake Mix—Manischewitz, Newark, N.J., and Aron Streit, N.Y.
  Add eggs

Matzos—Manischewitz, Newark, N.J., and Aron Streit, N.Y.
  Lunch snack with cheese, etc.

MEXICAN FOODS

Canned whole or diced green chilis—Ortega-Heublein, Inc., Hartford,
  Conn. 06101. Wash and dry for main dishes

Cracklings—Carmelita Provision Co., Monterey Park, Calif. 91754
  Pork skins cooked in fat and then salted

Taco Shells (pre-fried)—Lawry's Foods, Los Angeles, Calif. 90065
  Make tacos or eat as snacks

Tostadas (pre-fried)—Poco's-LaVencedora Products, Los Angeles, Calif.
  90063; Mission Mexican Foods, Van Nuys, Calif.
  Spread with margarine, salt and heat briefly for snacks

Ground dry shrimp (camaron)—Harmell Food Products, Los Angeles,
  Calif. 90062. Dried powdered shrimp for soups

ORIENTAL FOODS

Musubi Nori (dry seaweed) — Japanese import
Add to stews and soups

Miso-Shiru soy bean soup mix — Kikkoman Co., Tokyo, Japan
Five one-cup packets. Instant soup mix

Shirakiku Banshu Somen — Japanese alimentary paste
Looks like white spaghetti. Cookes in three minutes. Package divided
into five two-serving bundles

Cup Wonton Noodles — Kanebo Foods, Tokyo, Japan
Soup in its own cup. Cooks in three minutes

Chinaroni (water noodles) — Jan-U-Wine Foods, Los Angeles, Calif. 90051
Use for spaghetti, chow mein, fried noodles. Cooks in three minutes

Chuka Soba Alimentary Paste — Japanese import
Add to soup mixes. (The translated directions are worth the price of
the package)

Top Ramen Soups — Nissin Foods, Gardena, Calif. 90249
Add vegetables and more meat for a hearty dinner

Smack Noodles Soup — Like Top Ramen Mix

Cup O' Noodles — Nissin Foods
Instant meal in a cup

Jan-U-Wine Chow Mein Noodles — Snack, or base for stew, or soup
topping

Yee Fu Mein Soup Base — Maruchan, Inc., Los Angeles, Calif. 90030
Japanese product

**Large dried mushrooms are occasionally found packaged in the Oriental
Foods section of the market**

7

Of Course You Can:
Drying Your Own Backpack Foods

. . . Backpacking for days.
Found! New evidence of man:
Plastic container . . .

Our pioneer forefathers and the native Indians had at least two things in common . . . an appreciation of the land and its bounty, and a knowledge of preserving that bounty by the process of dehydration. Dried seeds and grains, dried fruits, corn and beans, dry meat in the form of jerky were all staples to be carefully stored against the time of famine during late winter.

Your own "time of famine," near the end of a long trail, can be avoided in the very same way—by drying your own backpack food. You need heat and moving air. This basic principle is relatively easy to achieve.

Stretch *fiberglass* window screening over a wooden frame (Never let drying foods touch metal.) Hang it near a hot water heater, a furnace outlet, or under the cook stove hood. The combination of low temperature (95°-110°) with an air flow will preserve the foods. Frequent stirring and rearranging will give proper exposure during the drying process.

If you live in a dry climate like the southwestern United States, you are lucky. A warm day (90°-100°) should be your signal to prepare food for a sun dryer:

1—Shallow-line a cardboard box with aluminum foil to reflect heat from under the food.

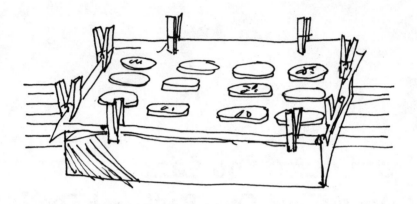

2—Stretch a long length of well-washed nylon net, mosquito net, cheesecloth, or a Dacron marquisette sheer curtain over the top of the box, and fasten securely around the top with spring clothes pins.

3—Place the prepared food on the fabric. Cover with the other end of the fabric (held above the food by the ends of the clothespins), fasten at the corners with more clothespins.

4—Put in a sunny spot, preferably in front of a wall, to reflect heat.

5—DO NOT leave outside overnight. The food will absorb moisture and defeat the gain you made during the day.

Leafy foods like parsley and celery leaves will be crisp in a few hours if the sun is hot enough. By cutting away the thick ribs from Romaine lettuce, beet tops, spinach, kale, chard and other greens, they too will soon by dry for storage. The ribs take longer to dry. Vegetables like carrots, celery, zucchini and cucumber should be sliced no less than 1/4 inch thick. They can dry paper thin and this makes them difficult to remove from the fabric. Dry bean sprouts and dry shredded cabbage will put the finishing touch to a vegetable stew. Use bouillon or a packaged soup mix as a base.

If the weather doesn't cooperate, your oven can be an ideal food dryer, though gas and electric heat must be treated differently. In a gas oven the pilot light helps to circulate the warm air.

Gas Oven Drying:
   1—Replace the oven light with a 150-watt light bulb. This is your heat source. DO NOT turn on the oven.
   2—Cover the oven racks with washed cheesecloth or other washed sheer fabric.
   3—Cover the food nearest the light (keep the top oven rack about five inches away) with a paper towel to keep it from getting scorched.
   4—Prop the oven door open a fraction of an inch with a multi-folded paper towel or hot pad to allow moisture to escape.
   5—Turn on the light for heat. Rotate food from one level to another and from front to back so it will all dry uniformly.

An *Electric Oven* can be used, but needs careful attention. After the food has been placed on the oven racks, turn the heat regulator to the lowest setting and leave the door open. Rotate the foods often and keep testing for brittleness. Be careful not to over-dry and scorch.

Instead of turning on the electric oven you can use the 150-watt bulb for heat, and proceed as above.

If you do not wish to tie up the oven racks, you can stretch cheesecloth over shallow baking pans, fasten with clothespins, arrange the food to be dried and place on the oven racks. These can be removed easily when you wish to use the oven.

Warning: Do not forget to return the *oven light* for regular baking. An ordinary light bulb could explode in the intense heat!

Electric Dryers are desirable and efficient, and well worth the time to construct if you are handy, or to buy if you are not. If you plan to do lots of food drying, the electric dryer will save time, because it will handle a greater volume of food in a shorter time.

Several publications give instructions on how to make your own electric dryer:
   1—Cooperative Extension Service, Washington State University, Pullman, Wash. 99163
   2—Extension Services, Utah State University, Logan, Utah 84322
   3—"Dry It, You'll Like It" by Gen Macmanimun, Fall City, Wash. 98024

To purchase an electric dehydrator, write:
   1—Sun-King Manufacturing, 126 N.E. 28th, Portland, Ore. 97232
   2—Retsel Corp., Mc Cammon, Idaho 83250

3—Mothers General Store, Box 506, Flat Rock, N.C. 28731
4—Make-it-yourself kit: Living Foods Dehydrator, P.O. Box 546, Fall City, Wash. 98024

Books available describing construction of various dryers:
1—"Home Canning," Sunset Books, Lane Publishing Co., Menlo Park, California 94025
2—"How To Dry Fruits and Vegetables At Home" by the Food Editors of Farm Journal, Doubleday and Co., Garden City, NY
3—"Dry It, You'll Like It" by Gen Macmanimun, Fall City, Wash. 98024

The above books also describe methods of drying a great variety of foods.

Some experts advocate blanching, steaming or sulfuring to preserve food color and halt oxidation. Others simply dry the foods "as is," and are not too concerned about the visual qualities. However, some vegetables can be very tough and refuse to rehydrate. Steaming (preferred) or blanching will overcome this problem at camp. Green beans are a good example. Dried beans should be thoroughly cooked, or you will use too much time and stove fuel trying to cook them at camp.

If the drying temperature is too high there is a danger of moisture being removed too fast. This causes a condition known as "case hardening" which is a hardening of the outer cells of the product. It prevents water vapor from diffusing from the inner cells, and the product will spoil. If the product has case-hardened, it will remain heavy after drying. If the temperature is *too low* to begin with, the product will sour.

When the weather is excessively humid, nothing will dry satisfactorily. Don't waste a rainy day on a food dehydration project.

Storage

The safest place to store your dried food is in the freezer. Light is an enemy of dried food, causing it to fade and deteriorate, so keep it in the dark.

Use jars with tight-fitting lids, or package the dried foods in plastic bags and place in coffee cans with plastic lids. Neither the bulk nor energy-yielding properties of vegetables are affected by drying. The smaller the pieces, the faster they dry, and the better color, flavor and nutritional value. If they are stored in a dark, cool, dry place, most dry foods should be good for a year. Carrots, onions and cabbage deteriorate rapidly, however, and have a shelf life of about six months.

Be sure you label food packages with the name and date of packaging. Remember to check your dry food often to see that it remains dry. If mold develops, discard it.

Almost anything edible can be dried for later use. Such things as whole eggs (whipped), low-fat cottage cheese, cooked meats, fresh vegetables, and cooked uncreamed casseroles can be enjoyed at the most remote campsite. Fruits and vegetables selected should be in the peak of condition. Immature foods will be weak in color and flavor, over-mature vegetables are tough and woody, over-ripe fruits tend to spoil before they can be dried.

Vegetables

Vegetables which have been flavorably combined, put in a blender, and then dried as "leather" are useful and quick-cooking additions to sauce mixes, stews and creamed soups.

Put 1/4 cup water in a blender. Add cut-up vegetables, cover and puree. Spread on plastic wrap, dry by one of the methods discussed earlier, break into pieces and store for future use.

- For a plain bouillon base, combine celery, onion, green pepper and parsley.
- For a more complete food, puree:
  1 small onion
  1 fresh tomato
  1 stalk of celery plus leaves
  2-3 sprigs of parsley
  1/2 cup cooked chicken
  Dash of sage, salt and pepper

Vegetable leathers can be dried by spoonfuls smoothed out to about 1/4" thick.

Variations: Cooked beef and oregano. Ham and marjoram. Additions of chili powder, garlic clove, *or* prepared mustard.

To thicken a beef-based soup, add "leathered" carrots, potatoes, or cabbage shreds.

A succotash of corn and lima beans would be enhanced with a "leather" of eggs, catsup, onion, green chili peppers, salt and pepper.

A good rule to follow when making any leather . . . if it tastes good in the blender, it will taste twice as good at camp. Before drying, sample and make additions till the combination pleases you.

The quickest and easiest way to prepare your own vegetables for drying is to purchase them frozen. Look for those that take the shortest cooking time. Birdseye brand puts out "five-minute vegetables." These include a good selection: Broccoli, peas, asparagus, corn, green beans, limas, and peas and carrots. Squashes do not dehydrate very "gracefully" after they have been frozen. However, they are easy to dry fresh.

Commercially frozen vegetables have been blanched to hold color and stop enzyme action. Blanched vegetables require less soaking, because they have been cooked briefly in boiling water or steam. Frozen vegetables are merely spread out and dried like fresh vegetables.

To rehydrate vegetables at camp, barely cover with water, bring to a boil, cover and remove from the heat for 10-15 minutes. You can add instant bouillon to the soaking water for more flavor. After rehydrating, return the vegetables to the heat and cook till barely fork tender. It is better to add more water than to start out with too much water.

Avoid drying strong vegetables such as cauliflower, cabbage, or onion with other foods unless you wish to combine them anyway. Milder foods will take on their pungent flavor.

Peppers add a lot to casserole combinations. Green and red sweet peppers dry and rehydrate very quickly when cut into 1/4" cubes. The long green mild chili peppers can be dried out of the can. (Look in the Mexican section), but are about half as expensive if purchased fresh. They do require special preparation: Wash the chilis, then, one at a time, pierce the stem end with a long-tined fork. This is your handle. Hold directly in a high gas flame to char the skin. When all surfaces are thoroughly blistered and burnt, place the chili in a plastic bag to steam while you char the next one. Leave them in a tightly closed bag for about 10 minutes after finishing the last pepper. Then, slip the skin from the chilis under running water. Cut off the stem end, split, remove the seeds and veining. Cut into 1/2" to 1" strips to dry. If they are cut too narrow, you will end up with "strings."

Dry Your Own Seasonings: Dry onion rings separately from other foods and be sure to place them on cheese cloth or paper towels to avoid contaminating the drying racks. Wash the cloth before using for other foods. Crush before storing, while still warm.

Parsley and celery leaves dry quickly. Wash and pat dry on a turkish towel before laying out to dry.

Freshly dried herbs give the best flavor. Use marjoram with ham, basil with beef, dill with fish, and mint leaves for a refreshing tea to go with dessert.

Drying Tomatoes: Canned tomato paste dries well. Spread evenly (don't thin out the edges) on plastic wrap or the inside of an opened plastic bag fastened to a cookie sheet with tape so the edges of the plastic won't curl. When dry on one side, peel from the plastic and turn over on a paper towel to complete drying. Break into chunks and store in bags, one can to each bag for easy measuring later. Keep them in a sealed Ziploc plastic bag in the refrigerator or freezer. Use them for sauces and as flavoring in soups and dinner combinations.

Tomato leather is made by combining peeled firm tomato chunks with fresh celery slices, parsley, onion and lemon juice pureed in a blender. Dry on plastic wrap as previously described.

Fresh tomato slices and wedges also dry easily for camp use.

Salad

Using cold stream water, rehydrate cabbage and carrot shreds. Drain if necessary, using any excess water in your one-pot meal. Top with pure lemon juice crystals (Reese brand), crushed dried lemon slices, or dried pulp that has been squeezed from citrus fruits. Add salt and pepper.

Stir well and return to the cold stream until dinner is ready.

Variation: Combine rehydrated cabbage, parsley, tomato slices and cottage cheese. Top with cooking oil, lemon juice crystals, salt, pepper.

Dry foods take up a lot less room than fresh ones. This makes measuring proper amounts difficult. After drying a box of frozen vegetables, measure to find out how much to plan for portions when making up food packages. A 10 oz. box of frozen peas will serve two to three when mixed with other ingredients.

Remember: Any vegetable enjoyed *raw* does not have to be cooked to a mush. Leave it a bit crunchy!

Tips on Drying Fresh Vegetables

- Artichokes—Use only tender hearts. Cut into 1/4" slices to dry.
- Asparagus—Use tender tips only. Wash well. Cut large tips in half.
- Green Beans—Use stringless varieties. Cut lengthwise or in 1" slices. *Note:* Green beans are tough. Steam 10-15 minutes before drying.
- Dried beans—Cook before drying, or they will take too long at camp.
- Bean Sprouts—Wash, blot dry on a towel before spreading to dry.
- Beets—Cook as usual. Cool, peel, cut into 1/4" strips for drying.
- Beet Greens: *See Spinach.*
- Broccoli—Use only flower heads. Quarter stalks lengthwise, but not clear through head to speed drying.
- Brussel Sprouts—Use small tight heads. Cut in half, lengthwise through stem.
- Cabbage—Remove outer leaves. Quarter and slice in 1/4" strips.

- Carrots—Use fresh, crisp, tender carrots. Scrub with a stiff brush. Trim and slice, dice or shred. Can be combined with cabbage.
- Cauliflower—Use small flowerettes. Cut in quarters or slice 1/4" thick.
- Celery—Trim stalks. Scrub well. Slice diagonally 1/4" thick. Dry the leaves and use, crumbled, for seasoning.
- Chayote (Mexican Squash)—Slice 1/4" thick after cutting in half.
- Corn—Cook on the cob until milk no longer runs from kernels. Cut from cob to dry. Spread on plastic wrap first, then transfer.
- Cucumber—Slice 1/4" thick. Be sure to peel if the product has been waxed to preserve it.
- Eggplant—Wash, trim, cut into 1/4" slices after quartering. Peeling is not necessary.
- Jerusalem Artichoke—Scrub thoroughly. Slice 1/4" thick. These can take the place of potatoes, and cook quickly.
- Mushrooms—Wash carefully. Discard woody stalks. Slice 1/4" lengthwise.
- Okra—Wash, trim, and slice crosswise in 1/4" pieces.
- Onions—Remove "paper" shell. Slice 1/4" thick. DO NOT DRY with other foods. Crumble before storing.
- Parsley—Wash well. Shake water off. When dry, crumble leaflets from tough stems.
- Peas—Shell. These need to be steamed three minutes to hasten cooking at camp.
- Peppers—Red or green. Wash, remove seeds and partitions. Cut into 1/4" rings or cubes.
- Potatoes—Wash and peel. Cut into 1/4" shoe strings or slices. Potatoes will darken. Sprinkle with lemon juice or ascorbic acid (canning aid) or steam three to five minutes before drying.
- Spinach and Greens—(Kale, chard, mustard, beets, Romaine lettuce, etc.) Wash thoroughly. Place each leaf face down on a cutting board. Cut alongside the center rib and remove it. Ribs take longer to dry and can best be used at home in soups or stews. The leaves dry very quickly.
- Squash—(pumpkin) Banana, Hubbard. Wash, slice into 1" strips. Remove seeds and pulp. Cut into cross strips 1/4" thick. If any pieces have darkened when drying, discard them.
  Clean and dry the seeds to be roasted for trail snacks.

- Squash—(Summer, crookneck, patty pan, zucchini) Wash and trim. Cut into 1/4" slices. Zucchini is excellent to eat dry, if the slices have been salted before drying.
- Tomatoes—Cherry- Wash, cut in half. Place skin side down to dry. Large, ripe, firm. Wash, cut in wedges, but not clear through the skin. Place skin side down to dry. Or, slice 1/4" thick to dry on plastic wrap. It is not necessary to peel tomatoes.
- Powdered Vegetables: After drying, grind fine in a blender or seed mill. Add to instant bouillon or broth packets for a quick hot drink.
- Soup Mixture—At home, combine a variety of dry vegetables. At camp add rice, macaroni, and/or dry cooked meat.

Indian Traveling Food

Zuni Indians prepare corn by drying and toasting, grinding and toasting again, and grinding again to a very fine flour. This is combined with meat that has been dried and ground into meal, chili powder and salt. Combine one teaspoonful with 2 cups water to make a thick and satisfying drink.

Apache Indians make a snack by finely grinding parched corn into meal and mixing it with ground sunflower seeds, walnuts, piñon nuts, or parched pumpkin seeds. This is eaten by the pinch, or baked into bread.

Taos Indians roast pumpkin seeds by first drying them in the sun, then placing the seeds in a bowl. Enough vegetable oil is added to lightly coat them. Salt is added and they are well stirred. The oiled seeds are spread on a tray and placed in a 250° oven, and stirred occasionally till they have turned brown.

Information from: *American Indian Food and Lore* by Carolyn Niethammer, Macmillan Pub. Co., New York 1974

Fruits

The high sugar content in fruits makes them easier to preserve, but it usually takes longer to dry them. When "dry," fruit contains more calories than when fresh, because of the concentrated natural sugar. Most fruits are considered "dry" when still pliable. Be sure to store air tight in the refrigerator or freezer.

The color of fruits will be enhanced if they have been treated. Ascorbic acid crystals can be purchased in the market canning section. They are found under brand names such as A.C.M., manufactured by Pfizer, Inc., N.Y. 10017, and others. Lemon juice crystals are convenient to use. Look in the gourmet or seasonings section. Fresh lemon or orange juice is also good for preserving color.

At camp, you can plump fruit by covering it with water, bringing to a boil, then simmering five minutes. A dash of salt will improve flavor, as will lemon juice crystals, a little lemonade mix, dried lemon slices, or a piece of leathered citrus pulp that has been re-covered when squeezing fresh oranges, lemons, or grapefruit. After removing the seeds, spread the pulp on plastic wrap and dry as for fruit leather.

If you have access to a seed mill try *Dried Berry Jam:*

Use blackberries, strawberries, etc. Dry the clean berries. They will be very hard. Put through a seed mill and package.

At camp: Add a small amount of hot water, stir and allow to steep. Sweeten with sugar or honey. Great on pancakes.

Cranberry juice can be carried to camp in the same way. Dry the cranberries, then put through a seed mill. (A blender will do, but will not powder the berries quite as fine.) *At camp*, add water for a juice. Cranberry flour is also tasty when added to stewing apples or apple sauce leather. Cranberry leather made from fresh berries is also a good way to carry it.

Dried banana slices are good as is, but variations are fun. Top fresh slices with cinnamon, nutmeg, toasted sesame seeds, chia seeds, toasted hulled sunflower seeds. Press the seeds into the fresh slices so they won't stray when dry. Brown sugar also can be used, but tends to caramelize onto the drying rack instead of staying on the banana slices.

Canned pineapple slices are packed in a syrup that gives them a sweetness not found in the fresh fruit. To dry, drain well in a sieve for an hour or two. Place on clean nylon net or cheesecloth and turn often.

By cutting fruits into small pieces and combining them to dry, you have the makings of a fruit stew. At camp add water, brown sugar and a little margarine for a pancake topping. Simmer a few minutes to blend the flavors. Apples, pineapple, and chopped walnuts are a good start.

To plump prunes: Cover with water and add orange juice crystals (Start, Tang). Leave overnight in a cold stream.

Fruit Leathers

"Leathers" are simply fruits cut up and placed in a blender or food grinder using the finest blade to make a smooth puree. If necessary, you could use a potato masher for softer fruits like peaches and plums. The puree is dried on plastic wrap that has been fastened to a flat surface. When the fruit can be pulled away from the wrap it is ready to be stored. Here is how you can do your own:

Place prepared fruit, a cup at a time, into a blender. Add a small amount of water if necessary to start the action. Puree till smooth. Add sweetening if desired (brown sugar, white sugar, Karo syrup, honey, molasses, bananas or dates). If the combination tastes good in the blender it will be delicious as leather.

Line jelly roll pans or cookie sheets with plastic wrap (or a plain plastic bag slit open), securing the edges with tape to prevent it from curling into the puree. Spread evenly in pans, leaving the edges thicker for easier handling later.

Dry according to your preference (sun, oven, dryer). Rotate the pans often to allow even drying when using the oven or electric dryer. When you can peel the leather from the plastic wrap, it is ready to roll and store. It will keep on a shelf about a month, in the freezer for a year.

Fruit leathers can be shaped into individual "balls" for easy trail handling by cutting the finished leather into one-inch strips, rolling, and wrapping individually in plastic wrap squares. Do not make them too big. A diameter about the size of a quarter is just right.

Leather sweetened with white sugar will often dry crispy. It is easily crushed to dissolve in hot water for cereal or pancake topping. Add it to hot tea for a flavorful drink.

An easy leather can be made from canned applesauce. With the addition of cinnamon or nutmeg and lemon juice it is delicious. Chopped nuts, flavorings (almond, vanilla, mint) and seeds (chia, sesame) are also interesting variations.

Canned mincemeat dries into a pemmican-type trail food.

PRICKLY PEAR LEATHER

The fruit from the prickly pear family of cactus makes delicious leather. Wash well. Scrub away spines by holding fruit with tongs and using a stiff brush. Force the pulp through a food mill. This strains out the skin and seeds. Add lemon juice for color retention. Spread on plastic wrap and dry. A blender is not necessary.

APPLE LEATHER

(If you prefer to peel your apples, save and dry the peeling separately to add to cooked cereals, granola, or pancake mix.)

Wash, core, chop apples. Place a few chunks and a tablespoon of lemon juice in a blender. Turn on and keep adding small amounts of apple. Also add honey or corn syrup to taste.

When the mixture is like thick applesauce, spread evenly on plastic wrap fastened to a cookie sheet with tape.

To make a *Half and Half Roll*: Leave one portion plain. Sprinkle cinnamon or other spice over the rest.

Wrap and store when dry enough to peel from the wrap.

Other Fruit Leather Suggestions:

Berries—including strawberries, raspberries and blackberries (seeds removed).

Apricot, plum, peach, nectarine—Wash. Do not peel. Cut up and pit. Add lemon juice to improve color.

Strawberry-Rhubarb—Combine:

   3 cups cut-up rhubarb
   3/4 cup sugar
   1/4 cup water

Simmer this mixture 8-10 minutes.

Add: 2-1/2 cups cut-up strawberries

Puree in a blender.

Cranberry Leather: Combine in a blender:

   1 one-pound package of fresh cranberries which
      have been washed and sorted.
   2 oranges, peeled and seeded.
   1 cup sugar

Puree till smooth

Think of this one during the holidays when fresh cranberries are available. They can be stored in the freezer till ready to be made into leather.

   Variation: Add apples instead of oranges.

Fruits

Tips on drying fruits:
- Apples—Peel and core. Cut into 3/8" slices or rings. To prevent browning, dip in a solution of 2-1/2 tsp. ascorbic acid crystals in one cup water. (Or lemon juice and water.) Dry the peel, too.
- Apricots—Wash. Remove pit, and cut in 1/4" slices. Do not peel. Dip in ascorbic acid solution (*see apples*).
- Bananas—Use ripe firm fruit. Peel and trim. Slice 1/4" thick.
- Berries—Use firm berries. Wash. Cut strawberries in half or slice large ones. Use ripe, firm blueberries, raspberries, etc.
- Cantaloupe—(honeydew or muskmelon). Use ripe fruit. Peel and cut into 1/2" slices.
- Cherries—Sort and wash firm fruit. Cut in half and remove pit.
- Cranberries: Wash, sort, slice in half.
- Figs—Use ripe fruit that is ready to fall into your hand from the branch. Wash. If small, leave whole; if large, cut in half.
- Grapes—(seedless varieties). Wash and sort. Cut closely packed stems into small bunches and leave fruit on the stem to dry.
- Nectarines and Peaches—Wash, cut in half, remove pit. Peel if desired. Cut into eighths or 1/4" slices. Dip in ascorbic acid.
- Oranges—(also grapefruit, lemons, limes) Select firm, ripe fruit. Peel and dry the peeling separately. Slice across the fruit in 1/4" slices to expose juice cells. Use crumbled dry peel for flavoring stewed fruits, etc.
- Papaya—Peel ripe fruit. Cut into 1/4" slices.
- Pears—(Bartletts are best) Wash, core, cut into 1/4" slices. Treat with ascorbic acid to prevent darkening.
- Pineapple—(Or use canned, drained slices.) Use very ripe fruit. Cut into lengthwise wedges. Remove core if desired. Dry with the peel side down till the juice no longer runs. Cut from peel to finish drying.
- Prunes and Plums—Use very ripe fruit. Cut in half, remove pit. Cut in slices for quicker drying. Place on plastic wrap for initial drying.
- Rhubarb—Use ripe fruit. Trim. Cut crosswise in 1/4" slices. If very tough, blanch or steam for a few minutes before drying.

Dried Meats

You can dry the white meat of chicken or turkey, beef, or ham. The method of drying depends on how you want to use it.

For Jerky: Choose the leanest beef (flank or round steak), and partially freeze to make slicing easier. Trim away all fat. It can become rancid very quickly. Slice about 1/2" thick. If you like it chewy, cut the meat with the grain; if you like it brittle, cut across the grain. Lay the strips of meat in a shallow pan in rows. If there is to be more than one layer, make the second one lie the other way for easier handling later. Pour the marinade over, moving the strips to allow it to touch all the meat. Cover with a plastic film, laying it on the meat to force out as much air as possible. Be sure all the meat is covered with marinade.

Leave in the refrigerator overnight. Drain and pat dry with paper towels. Lay the strips over oven racks or the barbeque grill to dry. Do not allow the pieces to touch. When dry, store in a tightly covered jar or sealed plastic bag.

I like to dry my jerky in the sun, but the oven method or electric dryer works well. Rotate the racks several times to allow the meat to dry evenly in the oven or dryer. Remember, you are not cooking the meat, only drying it. Check it often.

Marinade: Combine:

1/3 cup Worcestershire sauce
1/4 cup soy sauce
1/2 tsp. each onion and garlic powder
1/4 tsp. pepper (optional)
1 tsp. seasoned salt

Vary the amounts to suit yourself. Thyme, cloves or bay leaves can be added, and red wine is a favorite addition.

BEEF

Slice or cube and dry any COOKED beef that is free of fat. A pot roast is ideal to use. If a steak is fried in Pam or other non-stick preparation, it can be cubed and dried. For a "smoky" flavor, dip cooked cubes of beef in soy sauce before drying.

Ground round can also be dried, but with care! A well-seasoned meat loaf makes a good addition to a spaghetti sauce. Blot as much fat as possible from slices of cooked meat loaf. Crumble and spread out on paper towels to dry. Replace the paper towels as they absorb grease. When dry, seal and store in the freezer till ready to pack.

Seasoned hamburger can be prepared ahead of time by first frying and draining the fat. Stir in a dry taco, enchilada, spaghetti, or sloppy joe mix. Combine thoroughly before spreading on paper towels to dry. Do not plan to carry cooked ground meat more than a few days. It quickly deteriorates if not refrigerated.

HAM

You do not need a marinade to dry a fully cooked ham. Trim away all fat, cut into strips or cubes, dry on paper towels or cheese cloth so any beads of oil can be absorbed. Store in the refrigerator in jars with tight-fitting lids. One and a half pounds of ham will make about 1/2 pound of dry ham. When dry, ham is very salty, so use it sparingly. It is good for a trail snack when eaten with dried fruit. To combine with vegetables for a one-pot meal, rinse with hot water first to remove some of the salt. It is also good added to pancake mixes and scrambled eggs.

Occasionally markets will package "ham seasoning." You often can find generous chunks of pure ham. Trim, cube and dry. Use the scraps to season a pot of lima beans or split pea soup for home use.

POULTRY

Stew a chicken till the meat falls from the bones. Cut the meat into 1/2" cubes (or smaller) and dry on paper towels to absorb any fat. The cubes can be dusted with salt, poultry seasoning, garlic or onion salt, and marjoram before drying.

Turkey left-overs are excellent when dried. The white meat is more acceptable than the dark. However, a combination of both is good.

Hint: Crumble dry meats in the blender for quicker rehydration. Measure before crumbling for correct recipe use.

FISH

Be sure to dry fish alone on paper towels that can be discarded to avoid having the flavor creep into everything else you dry.

Clean and cut fresh fish into 1/2" cubes. Dip in soy sauce or lemon juice. Dry with plenty of air circulation.

Or, you can use a fish marinade:

1/4 cup soy sauce
1 tsp. honey
Salt and pepper

Marinate several hours before drying.

Rehydrated fish can be substituted for tuna in your favorite recipe.

Water Packed tuna and shrimp dry well. Drain, spread on paper towels and change towels to speed drying.

Small Frozen Cooked Cleaned Shrimp can be dried right out of the bag. Remove as much ice as possible before spreading on paper towels. Use in any tuna recipe. When rehydrated, shrimp cooks quickly, so add to the recipe at the last minute.

DRIED COTTAGE CHEESE

Choose low-fat cottage cheese for drying. It can be added to Stroganoff dishes in place of sour cream mix. It is also good when rehydrated along with dried fruit or fruit leather for a dessert. It also can be flavored with gelatin crystals (Cherry Jello) or dried parsley or celery leaves for variety.

To dry: Spread on plastic wrap and dry until it can be peeled from the wrap. Remove the plastic, turn the cottage cheese over on it and dry the other side.

Whirl in a blender to break up the chunks. Return to the drying pan if necessary.

Store the cottage cheese in the freezer and use early on the trail. When rehydrating, leave enough room for it to expand, and add more water as it "grows."

8

Day's End:
Dinners from Your Own Dried Foods

. . . We've been friends too long
Persistent companion.
Loyal mosquito . . .

A backpacking friend says, "We always start supper with a couple of packets of instant soup. After a long day's march it is amazing what one little cup of soup can do to bolster the spirits!" Soup warms you up, adds necessary liquid, and helps ward off exhaustion. It also gives you something to enjoy while waiting for dinner to cook.

How to rehydrate your dry foods: Place the contents of the meal (pre-packaged at home) in a cooking pot. Add water to barely cover, and bring to a rolling boil. Remove from the heat, cover tightly with a lid, and let set 10-15 minutes. Return to the heat and simmer till done. DO NOT OVERCOOK! Pre-cooked casseroles need only thorough rehydration. You might want to wrap the pot in a towel and then a sweater or jacket to keep the contents hot. (Don't let your nylon jacket touch the hot pot!)

Vegetables like shredded carrots and cabbage are delicious raw, after they have soaked in cold water. Add cut-up dried fruit and seeds. Peanut butter, thinned with a little dry milk and water, honey or jam, makes a good salad dressing. Add toasted hulled sunflower or pumpkin seeds, chia or poppy seeds for a change of texture.

101

Never discard excess liquid from cooked foods. Drink it to get all the nutrients. If you have a small cook pot, start with enough water to barely cover the rehydrated food. Add more water as needed, stirring the contents occasionally.

Remember, high mountain altitude causes water to boil at a lower temperature, foods take longer to cook, and the cooking time has to be increased on recipes.

Your own dried cooked meats will often take longer to rehydrate than the vegetables. If you don't mind a chewy texture, rehydrate the meat with the vegetables. Otherwise, start the meat first, and add the vegetables a few minutes later. The dry meat can be "chopped" in the blender, and the smaller pieces will rehydrate quicker.

If you do not want to dry your own potatoes, use the dry potatoes from a casserole mix. Instant mashed potato flakes can be added to thicken a stew or vegetable combination.

Food boredom is a recognized trail malady. Change the menu with one of the following:

Sour cream sauce mix, made according to directions, adds a change when used as a topping for casseroles and vegetable/meat combinations. It is a convenient way to avoid food repetition.

Another way to change an entree is to place a generous slice of cheese (jack, cheddar, Swiss) on the bottom of your bowl or plate before spooning in the hot mixture. Experiment with herbs and spices. They give lots of flavor at little expense.

Use bouillon as a seasoning to create a different taste. Search the foreign foods section for broth packets. Quick soup mixes can be the base for a wide variety of food combinations. Be sure to check the cooking times required. Add rice, macaroni, noodles, or fancy pasta shapes for a satisfying quick meal.

During the day, sugars and starches digest quickly and give energy when hiking demands it. Protein and fats digest more slowly and help maintain a constant flow of energy. At the end of a long day, a good hot meal will help to increase body heat and insure a comfortable nights' sleep.

If you get stuck, of course you can substitute freeze-dried or dehydrated meats and vegetables in the following recipes.

MIXES

You can save up to 50-percent if you make your own mixes, and they can be made in a few minutes. A bonus is the fact that they include no unnecessary additions or preservatives. The following combinations have a shelf life of several months if stored in the refrigerator:

BREADING

Combine crushed corn flakes or dried bread that has been ground up in a blender, salt, pepper, garlic and onion salt, dry parsley flakes. Use as a coating for fresh fish.

SEASONED SALT

Combine equal amounts of onion and garlic salt, regular salt, and paprika.

SALAD SEASONING MIX

(1/3 cup dry)

Combine:

>   **2 tbls. seasoned salt**
>   **2 tsp. each crushed basil, onion flakes, celery flakes,
>   parsley flakes, dillweed**
>   **1/2 tsp. each garlic powder, paprika**
>   **1/4 tsp. pepper**

Store in a tightly covered container.

At camp: Add to oil and lemon juice crystals a little at a time till it tastes to your liking, sprinkle dry over salad combinations, or sprinkle on rehydrated cottage cheese.

BASIC WHITE SAUCE MIX

Combine and sift thoroughly:
> **3/4 cup flour (unbleached if you can get it)**
> **4 tsp. salt**
> **1/2 tsp. pepper**
> **4 cups milk**

Cut in: **1 cup margarine (2 sticks)**

When the mixture is the texture of corn meal, store in a tightly covered container in a cool, dry place.

To make 1 cup medium white sauce, combine:
> **1/2 cup mix**
> **2/3 cup water**

Cook and stir over medium heat until the sauce comes to a boil. Continue simmering and stirring for 2-3 minutes.

Variations: Cheese—stir in 1/2 cup shredded cheese, 1/4 tsp. dry mustard. Curry—Stir in 1/2 tsp. curry powder. Egg—Stir in 1/2 cup dry egg powder and a pinch of dry parsley.

Use white sauce with vegetables, macaroni, rice, or meats.

BISCUIT MIX
(10-11 cups)

Combine:
> **8 cups all-purpose flour**
> **1-1/2 cups dry milk**
> **1/4 cup baking powder**
> **1 tbls. salt**

Add: **1 cup shortening**

Cut in shortening until mixture is very smooth and about the consistency of cornmeal. Store in the refrigerator in a tightly closed container until ready to use.

PANCAKES

Combine:
> **1 cup biscuit mix**
> **1/3 cup dry egg powder**
> **2 tsp. sugar**

At camp: Stir in 1/2 cup water. Bake on a greased frying pan.
6 medium pancakes

BANNOCK

Combine:
> **1 cup biscuit mix**
> **1/4 cup grated cheese**
> **1/4 cup raisins**

At camp: Add 1/3 cup water. Mix by hand till soft but not sticky. Place in a greased fry pan and bake, covered, over low heat. Turn when half done. Don't hurry it!

   Variation: Fry bacon, crumble into dough, use bacon grease for baking.

2 servings

PUDDING MIX

Combine thoroughly:
2 cups non-fat dry milk
1 cup granulated sugar
3/4 cup cornstarch
1/2 tsp. salt
Cover tightly and store in a cool dry place.

VANILLA PUDDING

At home, combine: 1 cup plus 2 tbls. pudding mix, and a tiny piece (1/4") of vanilla bean found in the seasoning section of the market.

At camp: Place the mix in a sauce pan. Add 2 cups water. Boil gently, stirring constantly, for 2-3 minutes. Add 2 tbls. margarine. Enjoy warm or chilled.

CHOCOLATE PUDDING

Omit margarine. Add pieces of chocolate bar and stir till melted. Or, add chocolate bits.

BUTTERSCOTCH PUDDING

Add butterscotch morsels and stir till melted.

EASY CREAM SAUCE

At home, combine:
1 tsp. dry onion flakes
1/4 tsp. dry parsley flakes
1/4 tsp. dry celery leaves
1 tbls. flour
1/4 tsp. salt, dash of pepper
1/3 cup dry milk

At camp: Combine the dry ingredients with 1 cup water using a fork or a wire whip. Cook over medium heat until thickened, stirring constantly.

Serve mixed with rehydrated vegetables.

Variation: Add 1/4 cup cubed cheese (jack, cheddar, American) and stir until melted.

1 cup

TOMATO SAUCE

At home, combine:

1 tbls. dry onion flakes
1/2 tsp. oregano
1/2 tsp. sugar
2 tbls. flour
1 heaping tsp. instant beef bouillon (or 1 cube)
2-3 tbls. dry tomato "flour" (place dry tomato slices in
a blender) or use 1/2 can tomato paste leather
(see chapter on drying)

At camp: Melt 2 tbls. margarine in a cooking pot. Combine the dry ingredients with 1-1/2 cups water and add to margarine. Stir and simmer till thickened, about 5 minutes. Serve with beef and vegetables.

Variation: Melt cheese in the sauce.

1-1/4 cups

CREOLE SAUCE

At home, combine:

2 tsp. dry onion flakes
2 tbls. dry green pepper cubes
2 tbls. dry mushroom slices, crumbled
1/4 cup dry tomato slices, crushed
1/2 tsp. sugar

Also take **1 package brown or mushroom gravy mix.**

At camp: Rehydrate dry ingredients in hot water 10-15 minutes. Add 1 cup water and bring to a boil. Add gravy mix and cook till thickened. Serve over cooked rice or prepared instant potatoes.

Variation: Add t.v.p. and rehydrate with the vegetables to make bigger servings.

1-3/4 cups

HUSH PUPPIES MIX

At home, combine:
> **2 cups yellow corn meal**
> **1 cup flour**
> **4 tsp. baking powder**
> **2 tsp. salt**
> **3 tbls. sugar**
> **1/4 cup dry onion flakes**
> **3-4 tbls. dry egg powder**

At camp: Measure out one cup of the mixture. Add just enough water to make a thick dough. Drop by spoonfuls on a well-greased (very generously) hot skillet. Turn to brown both sides. sides.

3 meals' worth

EASY CREAMED DINNER

At home, combine:
> **2 tbls. flour**
> **1/3 cup dry milk**
> **1/2 tsp. salt, dash of pepper**

At camp: Melt 2 tbls. margarine in a saucepan. Combine the dry ingredients with 1 cup water. Add to margarine, stirring constantly until thickened. Allow to cook over low heat for 5 minutes, stirring occasionally. Add cubed cheese if you like.

Add rehydrated and cooked vegetables, canned fish, shrimp, chipped beef that has been rinsed in hot water to remove salt, or rehydrated meats. Serve over canned Chinese noodles, or cooked rice.

1 cup sauce

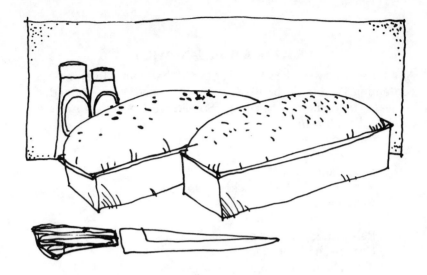

Breads as a Part of the Meal
BUTTERS

Sesame Seed—In a small pan brown 2 tbls. sesame seeds over medium heat till golden. Cool. Blend with 1/2 cup soft margarine and 1/2 tsp. garlic salt. Good to use for cooking fresh-caught fish.

Onion Butter—Blend 1/2 cup soft margarine with 2 tbls. onion soup mix. Spread on skillet-toasted French bread.

DINNER SKILLET TOAST

Use bread slices, English muffins, fruit breads, etc. Spread one side generously with margarine. Place spread side down in a medium hot skillet till lightly browned and the edges are crisp.

INDIAN FRY BREAD

At home, combine:
> **3 cups flour**
> **3 tsp. baking powder**
> **1 tsp. salt**

At camp, add: 1-1/2 to 1-2/3 cups water . . . just enough to form a biscuit dough consistency. Knead well until the dough is elastic and doesn't stick. (Have some extra flour available.)

For 7-8 inch rounds, use a piece of dough the size of a lemon. Pat by hand into a flat round shape. Fry in deep fat, turning once. The bread should be crisp on the outside. Serve hot.

CRACKER BREAD SANDWICH

As a base, use Swedish rye cracker bread that comes in a package containing 11″ rounds, or use Ry-Krisp, seasoned or unseasoned.

Heat a frying pan (with cover). Spread rye cracker with one or more of the following:

> Canned meat spread
> Liverwurst
> Dry salami
> Rehydrated turkey, chicken, ham, beef
> Rehydrated tomato slices
> Rehydrated zucchini slices
> Rehydrated, cooked mixed vegetables
> Crisp fresh carrot slivers
> Sliced hard-boiled egg

Top with slices of jack or cheddar cheese to cover the cracker. Place in a lightly greased fry pan, cover, and heat till cheese melts to hold the ingredients together.

BISCUIT MIX VARIATIONS

To the mixed dough add:

> **Fried bacon, crumbled**
> **Shredded sharp cheddar cheese**
> **Caraway seed**
> **Powdered sage**
> **Dry mustard, sparingly**
> **Toasted sunflower seeds**
> **Chopped nuts**
> **Dried orange peel flakes**
> **Finely chopped dry fruits**

The Optimus Mini-Oven fits on top of a backpack stove. It weighs 15-1/2 oz. Use it to make omelets made from dry egg powder, biscuits, small cake mixes (Cinch, Jiffy) and muffin mixes.

GRILLED DINNER SANDWICH

For each sandwich—Butter one side of a slice of bread (French is good). Place spread side down in a fry pan. Top with a slice of mozzarella cheese, 1-2 slices salami, and another slice of bread, buttered side up. When browned on one side, turn and brown the other.

Variations: Any sandwich can be grilled . . . tuna, chicken, luncheon meat, deviled ham, liverwurst, sliced cooked egg, cheese, etc. Banana with toasted sunflower seeds is great!

TASTY ENGLISH MUFFINS

Combine **1/2 cup margarine** with one of the following:

> **2 tsp. bouillon—chicken, beef, onion**
> **3-4 tsp. parmesan cheese (grated)**
> **1 tsp. chili powder**
> **1 tsp. dill weed, oregano, marjoram, basil, or thyme**
> **Dry parsley or celery flakes**
> **Celery, sesame, or poppy seeds**
> **Garlic or onion salt**

Spread on split muffin halves and place buttered side up in a heated skillet till margarine is melted.

8 halves

ENGLISH MUFFIN EGGS

At home, combine:
   1/4 cup dry mushroom slices
   1/2 cup dry tomato slices
   1 tsp. dry onion flakes
Also include:
   1/2 cup dry egg powder
   Salt and pepper
   2 English muffins

At camp: Rehydrate the mushroom package in cold water. Combine egg powder with scant 1/2 cup water which includes any extra liquid from rehydration. Combine all ingredients and pour into greased frying pan. Cook slowly, stirring often. Spoon mixture over warmed, buttered English muffins. (This is also good spooned into pita bread halves.)

2 servings

CORN FRITTERS

At home, combine:
   1/2 cup dry milk
   1/4 tsp. paprika
   1 tsp. salt
   1 tbls. sugar
   1-1/2 tsp. baking powder
   2 heaping tbls. dry egg powder
   1 cup flour (for a change, try whole wheat or rye)
Also include **1/2 cup dried frozen corn.**

   At camp: Rehydrate corn in 1 cup water for 10 minutes. Add corn and water to dry ingredients and mix well. (Add a little more water if needed.)

   Melt 1 tbls. margarine in a frying pan, and add to the batter. Fry by spoonfuls in a hot, greased fry pan, turning to brown.

   Variations: Add rehydrated bell pepper cubes, shredded cheese, chopped dry salami, parsley or celery or onion flakes.

2-3 servings

CORN BREAD DINNER

At home: Bake corn bread either by a mix or cookbook recipe, except add one or more of the following before baking:

Diced cooked bacon, rinsed chipped beef cut up, cooked ham-chicken-turkey cubes, left-over cooked vegetables such as green beans, peas, corn.

At camp: Split squares, spread with margarine and heat buttered side down in a covered skillet. Serve with hot soup or bouillon.

9-12 squares

CORN WITH PITA BREAD

At home, combine:

1 tsp. instant chicken bouillon
2 tsp. dry onion flakes
1/4 cup dry celery slices
1 tbls. dry green pepper cubes
1 pkg. dried frozen corn
1 tsp. bacon bits, or 2 tbls. dry ham cubes

At camp: If using ham, rinse in water to remove some of the salt. Rehydrate, then simmer till vegetables are barely cooked. Add more water only if needed. Spoon the corn mixture into pita bread halves that have been warming on the pot lid.

2-3 servings

ASPARAGUS WITH PITA BREAD

At home, combine:

3/4 to 1 cup asparagus tips (dry)
1 tbls. dry onion flakes
Small pinch of dry garlic flakes

Also include:

1 tbls. flour
1/2 cup dry milk
Pinch of thyme

At camp: Rehydrate asparagus package. Measure remaining liquid, and add hot water to make 1 cup. Add flour and dry milk package, and the liquid to the vegetables. Also add 1 tbls. margarine. Cook, stirring constantly till thickened. Add shredded cheddar cheese and stir till melted. Serve in pita bread halves.

2-3 servings

CAMP TACOS OR TOSTADAS

At home, combine:
> **1 pkg. TVP (textured vegetable protein)**
> **1 pkg. taco seasoning mix**

Also include:
> **1 pkg. pre-fried taco or tostada shells (1 doz.)**
> **Sharp cheddar or jack cheese**
> **12 tomato slices, dried**

At camp: Combine t.v.p. mix and 1 cup water. Bring to a boil and simmer according to seasoning mix directions. Rehydrate tomato slices in very little cold water. Cut cheese into thin strips. Spoon the filling into (or over) shell, top with tomato slices and cheese strips.

To add crunch—top with fresh carrot slivers. Fresh picked miner's lettuce or watercress is a good substitute for lettuce. A sour cream mix makes a good taco topping. Rehydrated cottage cheese makes an acceptable sour cream substitute.

10-12 servings

CAMPERS NACHOS

For this appetizer you will need:
> Frying pan
> Two foil pie pans that fit inside the frying pan
> 3-4 clothespins

You will also need:
> 1 pkg. Fritos Corn Chips (dip size)
> 2-3 cups shredded jack or cheddar cheese. (This can be
> prepared at home and carried in a plastic bag.)
> 1 can (4 oz.) diced green chilis (Ortega brand)

At camp: Spread a layer of overlapping corn chips in a foil pan. Place it in the frying pan. Sprinkle the chips evenly with cheese, then chilis. Cover with the second foil pan inverted, and fasten together with clothespins. Heat until cheese is melted. Eat and repeat!

Use any remaining corn chips as a base for a bean combination dinner and top it with any left-over cheese.

NEVER OVER-COOK CHEESE. When it is melted, it is "cooked." (Foil wrap could be used to line the frying pan and to use as a cover if you wish.)

DUMPLINGS

At home, combine:
> **1 cup Bisquick or your own mix (above)**
> **1/3 cup dry milk**

At camp: add 1/3 cup water. Mix and drop by spoonfuls into boiling liquid. Cook covered 20 minutes. Dumplings can be cooked in stew, soups and juicy fruit compotes to help make a meager meal more filling. (Thick pancake batter can be substituted.)

Salads

At home, combine:
> **Dry shredded cabbage**
> **Dry pineapple slices or pieces**
> **Raisins**

At camp: Rehydrate in cold water.

Make a dressing of margarine and lemon juice crystals or flavored fruit drink crystals, or peanut butter and honey or fruit jelly.

Variation: Dry carrot shreds, parsley flakes, peanuts.

CRUNCHY CHICKEN SALAD

At camp, combine:
> **3 cups dried and rehydrated chicken cubes**
> **3 medium thin-sliced fresh carrots, cut into strips**
> **1 cup chopped salted peanuts (or cashews, almonds)**
> **1/4 cup sesame seeds, toasted**

Dressing: 3 tbls. margarine, 1 tsp. sugar, 1/2 tsp. dry mustard, salt and pepper, and a pinch each of crushed dry parsley and celery leaves.

3-4 servings

Soups and Chowders

BASIC VEGETABLE SOUP

At home, combine:

2 rounded tsp. instant beef or chicken bouillon
1/2 cup crushed dried tomato slices
1/4 cup dry sliced celery
1/4 cup dry sliced carrots
1/4 tsp. dry parsley
2 tsp. dry onion flakes

At camp: Rehydrate, and simmer till vegetables are cooked. To this basic recipe add your choice of:

Dried cooked beef or chicken
Instant rice
Oriental alimentary paste (noodles or spaghetti)
   which takes 3 minutes to cook
Cheese cubes
Pasta (macaroni, noodles, shells, etc.)

For more tomato flavor, add 1/4 can of dried tomato paste leather. Beef or chicken based soup mix can be used instead of bouillon.

2-3 servings

SPLIT PEA SOUP

At home, combine:
>**2 pkgs. split pea soup mix**
>**2 tbls. dry celery slices**
>**1 tsp. dry parsley leaves**
>**1 tbls. dry onion flakes**
>**Dash of pepper**

Also include: 4-5 tbls. dried ham cubes, packaged separately.

At camp: Rehydrate ham cubes in hot water. Drain and discard liquid. Add ham to dry ingredients. Add water according to pkg. directions. Simmer according to package directions or till celery slices are done.

3-4 servings

SWISS POTATO SOUP

You will need:
>**1 pkg. Wyler's Potato Soup with Leek**
>**1/2 cup dry milk**
>**1/2 pkg. dried frozen peas**
>**1/2 cup Swiss cheese, shredded or cut into small pieces**
>**2 tsp. bacon bits**

At camp: Combine soup mix, dry milk and 3-4 cups water. Bring to a boil, add peas, and simmer 8-10 minutes. Stir in cheese and bacon bits.

2 servings

KIDNEY BEAN SOUP

At home, combine:
>**1 can (1 lb. 12 oz.) kidney beans that have been drained and dried**
>**1 tbls. each onion flakes, dry diced celery, and dry diced green pepper**
>**1/4 cup dried crushed tomato slices**
>**1 tsp. salt, dash pepper**
>**1 rounded tsp. instant beef bouillon**

At camp: Rehydrate, and then simmer in enough water to make a thin or thick soup, as desired.

2 servings

SPUD 'N HAM SOUP
(Ingredient amounts are variable)

To a pot of boiling water add:

> **Dried ham cubes that have been rinsed in hot water to remove excess salt**
> **Dried green chili pepper (or sweet pepper cubes)**
> **Dried onion flakes, parsley and celery leaves**
> **Large dollop of margarine**

Simmer till ham is rehydrated.

Add: **Dry powdered milk**
> **Dry potato flakes (sparingly, because they thicken as they cool)**
> **Salt and pepper**

Variation: Top each serving with cubed jack cheese and hulled toasted sunflower seeds. Ham-flavored Proteinettes (Creamette Co.) can be substituted for ham.

FRENCH ONION SOUP

At camp, you will need:

> **1 envelope onion soup mix**
> **2 tbls. margarine**
> **French bread**
> **Grated Parmesan cheese**

In a cooking pot place 3 cups water, onion soup mix, and margarine. Bring to a boil, then simmer 15 minutes.

To serve: Toast slices of French bread over flame, holding the slice with a fork or pointed stick. Put the bread in a bowl, and pour hot soup over the bread. Sprinkle generously with cheese.

Variation: Use plain or flavored croutons instead of French bread.

2-3 servings

CHICKEN SOUP

To a package of chicken-noodle soup add your choice of the following:

> Dry carrot slices or shreds
> Dry onion slices
> Shredded cabbage, dried
> Dry celery slices
> Dry tomato slices
> Dry potato flakes

HAM SOUP

At home, combine:

> **1 pkg. Wyler's Potato Soup with Leek**
> **1 pkg. Lipton's Mushroom Soup**
> **1/2 cup dry milk**

Also include:

> **1 can (2-1/4 oz.) deviled ham**

At camp: Combine mixes with 4 cups water and cook according to package directions. Stir in deviled ham.

3-4 servings

CHEESE CHOWDER

At home, combine:

> **1/4 cup each dry carrot and celery slices**
> **2 tbls. green pepper cubes**
> **1 tbls. dry onion flakes**
> **1 tbls. instant chicken bouillon**

Combine separately:

> **1 tbls. flour**
> **1/2 cup dry milk**
> **Salt and pepper**

Also include a 2" x 2" cube of cheddar cheese.

At camp: Heat 3 cups water to boiling. Add dry vegetables and rehydrate 10-15 minutes. Return to heat and simmer till vegetables are cooked. Add flour mixture and stir constantly till thickened. Add cut-up cheese, and stir till melted.

2 servings

OATMEAL SOUP

At home, combine:
> **2 tbls. dry onion flakes**
> **1/2 cup dry celery slices**
> **1 cup regular oatmeal**

Also take along:
> **1 tsp. instant beef bouillon**
> **2 tbls. margarine**

At camp: In a pot, heat margarine with onion, celery and oatmeal. Stir until oatmeal is lightly browned. Add 3 cups water and instant bouillon. Simmer 15-20 minutes. Add more water if necessary. Add salt and pepper to taste.

CHICKEN CHOWDER

At home, combine:
> **1 pkg. chicken noodle soup**
> **1/2 cup dried, cubed, cooked chicken**
> **1/2 pkg. dried frozen corn**

Also take along:
> **1/2 cup dry milk**
> **1/4 cup coffee lightener**

At camp: Add 3 cups water to soup package. Simmer 10-15 minutes. When chicken is rehydrated, add milk, stirring constantly. *Do not boil.*

  Variation: Add dried peas, or dried celery slices.

2-3 servings

RAMON SOUP

At home, combine:
> **3 pkgs. Lipton's Mushroom Cup-a-Soup**
> **6-8 dry greens (Romaine lettuce, chard, spinach, etc.)**
> **1 pkg. Oriental noodles (alimentary paste)**

Also take along:
> **1/2 cup dry cooked cubed chicken**

At camp: Measure 3 cups water into a pot. Add chicken and simmer till chicken is rehydrated, 10-15 minutes. Add soup mixture with greens and noodles, broken up. Simmer three minutes.

  Variation: Use tomato soup and dried cooked beef.

2 servings

CORN AND MUSHROOM CHOWDER

At home, combine:

Dry potatoes from a casserole mix
1 tbls. dry onion flakes
1/2 pkg. dried frozen corn
1/4 cup dry mushroom pieces

Also take along:

2 envelopes Lipton's Mushroom Cup-a-Soup
2/3 cup dry milk
2 tsp. bacon bits

At camp: Rehydrate dry vegetables, then simmer till tender. Add soup mixes, milk and bacon bits. Simmer till flavors are well blended. *Do not boil.*

2-3 servings

VEGETABLE CHOWDER

At home, combine:

2 tbls. onion flakes
1 cup potatoes, diced and dried (or use out of Betty
  Crocker casserole package)
1/2 cup sliced dried carrots
1 cup dried frozen lima beans

Also take along:

1 tsp. bacon bits
1 tbls. flour
1/2 cup dry milk

At camp: Rehydrate vegetable package. Add 1 cup water to dry milk package. Mix well. Cook vegetables till tender. Add milk mixture slowly, stirring constantly. Simmer 5 minutes.

Variation: Hash brown potato mix can be used instead of onions and potatoes.

3-4 servings

Eggs
DINNER OMELETS

At home, combine:

> **6 tbls. dry egg powder (or take along 3 eggs)**
> **1/3 cup dry milk**
> **2 tbls. coffee lightener**
> **1/2 tsp. salt, dash of pepper**
> **1/2 tsp. each parsley and celery flakes**
> **1 tsp. onion flakes**

At camp: Add: **1/3 cup lukewarm water and beat vigorously to dissolve the egg powder.**

To this, add your choice of:

> Cubed Swiss, jack or cheddar cheese
> Rehydrated vegetable
> Bacon bits or ham cubes

Melt 1 tbls. margarine in a frying pan. Add the egg mixture. Cover and cook slowly till set.

2 servings

Other Combinations:

> Cheese and chili powder
> Dried canned or frozen shrimp
> Dry salami, cut up, with dry tomatoes
> Parched corn and onion
> Toasted sunflower seeds

HAM-VEGETABLE OMELET

Combine and rehydrate:

> **Dry zucchini slices**
> **Dry Jerusalem artichoke slices**
> **Dry ham cubes, rinsed in hot water**

Cook these ingredients in a small amount of water. Add 1 tbls. margarine. Combine dry egg powder, dry milk, coffee lightener, salt, pepper. Pour over vegetables and ham. Cover and cook till eggs are set.

(Amounts are variable)

TVP SCRAMBLE

To boiled and drained t.v.p. (Proteinettes) add:
> **1 tsp. dry onion flakes**
> **1/2 tsp. salt, dash of pepper**

Combine and add:
> **2/3 cup dry egg powder**
> ` **2 tbls. dry milk**
> **1/2 cup water**

Add all ingredients to 2 tbls. melted margarine in a frying pan. Stir gently till eggs are set.

Variation: Add dried greens such as spinach, chard, kale.

2-3 servings

EGGS 'N RICE

At home, combine:
> **1-1/3 cups Minute Rice**
> **1/2 tsp. dill weed**
> **1 tbls. bacon bits**
> **Salt and pepper**

Also take: **2 fresh eggs or the equivalent dry egg powder**

At camp: Place rice in a cooking pot. Add 1-1/3 cups water and 1 tbls. margarine. Bring to a boil. Cover and remove from the heat 5-7 minutes. Return to heat. Break eggs over the mixture. Stir and cook till eggs are set. Top each serving with a slice of Swiss or jack cheese.

2 servings

CORN CRUNCH FRITTERS

At home, combine:
> **1 cup parched corn left whole or crushed**
> **2 heaping tbls. dry egg powder (or 2 eggs)**
> **1/3 cup flour**
> **1/2 tsp. baking powder**
> **Salt and pepper**

At camp: Heat 2 tbls. margarine in a skillet. Add enough water to the dry ingredients to make a thick batter. Fry by spoonfuls over medium heat, browning both sides.

Variation: Add bacon bits or dried ham cubes.

10-12 fritters

TVP Combos

Don't expect textured vegetable protein (tvp) to taste like hamburger. It really doesn't have much taste at all. By adding it to flavorful ingredients you are acquiring needed protein to keep up your energy.

Some brands require boiling before adding to other ingredients (Proteinettes), others ask only for a few minutes pre-soak (Plus Meat soy flour by Mrs. Filbert's). Armour's Burger Savor can be added without soaking. It has ingredients other than tvp, so choose carefully.

QUICK TVP COMBINATIONS

Add 1/2 cup prepared tvp to:
> **Any packaged soup mix**
> **Noodles**
> **Dry green pepper and onion**
> **Pinch of Italian seasoning**

Top with: **Cubed cheddar cheese**

To: **Rehydrated corn, mushrooms, tomato slices**
> **Dry onion**
> **Garlic chips**
> **Salt and pepper**

Top with: **Cubed Swiss cheese**

To: **Rehydrated sliced dried potatoes**
> **Rehydrated shredded diced beets**
> **Bacon bits, salt and pepper**

Top with: **Cubed jack cheese**

Proteinettes (ham or beef flavored) is a granular tvp product, and requires cooking before adding to other ingredients. However, if you are using macaroni, spaghetti, or noodles, both can be boiled at the same time. Use only as much water as necessary. Drain before adding to other ingredients.

Kraft or Golden Grain Macaroni and Cheese, Rice-A-Roni in various flavors, hamburger-helper-type products, brown gravy, cheese sauce, or white sauce mixes, and dry soup mixes are all enriched with the addition of tvp.

Cooked and drained ham-flavored Proteinettes can be added to scrambled eggs, instant potatoes or rice. Spaghetti or taco mixes can use the beef flavored tvp.

You can prepare your own soybean granules. For 1-1/2 cups cooked soy beans (before drying):

> Rinse 1/2 cup soy beans, sort, soak overnight in 1-1/2 cups water.
>
> Strain remaining liquid into a sauce pan. Discard loose skins.
>
> Add beans to the liquid, adding more water to cover beans.
>
> Cover pan and simmer till beans are tends, 3-4 hours.

Drain and dry by one of the methods described in the chapter on drying. "Chop" in the electric blender when mostly dry. Return to complete drying.

Store in a tightly sealed jar or plastic bag in the refrigerator or freezer till ready to package for a trip. Don't expect your tvp to look like the commercial kind. You won't need to color your product.

TVP SKILLET DINNER

1 pkg. Proteinettes (ham or beef)
2 pkgs. Lipton's Tomato Cup-a-Soup
1-1/3 cups Minute Rice
Salt and Pepper

At camp: prepare tvp as directed.

To 2 cups water add tvp and rest of ingredients. Bring to a boil, cover, and simmer on very low heat, 5 minutes. Add seasonings to taste.

2-3 servings

HAMMED MACARONI

Cook together in salted water and drain:

> **1/2 of an 8 oz. pkg. elbow macaroni**
> **1 pkg. ham-flavored tvp (Proteinettes)**

Add: **1 tbls. dry onion flakes**
> **1 cup water**
> **1/2 cup dry milk**
> **2" x 2" square of diced sharp cheddar cheese**
> **Salt and pepper**
> **Prepared mustard to taste (individual packet)**

Stir till cheese melts.

Variation: Add dry, rehydrated peas or carrots.

2-3 servings

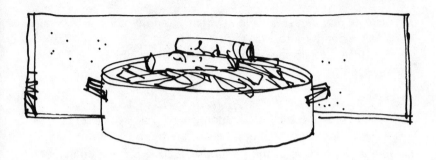

BACKPACK STEW

At home, combine:

    1 pkg. tvp (non-cook, just-soak kind)
    1 pkg. vegetable-beef soup mix
    1/4 cup dried sliced carrots
    1/4 cup dried green beans (Birdseye, 5-minute frozen)

At camp: Rehydrate, then simmer till vegetables are cooked.
  Variations:

    Add Bisquick dumplings.
    Add other dried vegetables to serve more.
    Add no-cook noodles (Mrs. Reis brand)
    Add instant rice.

2 servings

TVP JUMBLE

At home, combine:

    1 envelope tvp (non-cook kind)
    1 cup dry zucchini slices
    1/4 cup dry carrot slices
    1/4 cup dry celery slices
    1 tbls. dry onion flakes
    1 tsp. dry parsley flakes
    1/4 of a can of leathered tomato paste
    1/4 tsp. garlic chips
    Salt and pepper

Also include: **Grated Parmesan cheese.**

At camp: Rehydrate all ingredients but cheese. Cook until carrots and celery are tender. Sprinkle each serving with cheese.

2 servings

TVP STROGANOFF

Boil: **1 pkg. (3 oz.) beef flavored tvp (Proteinettes)**
With: **1 pkg. (7 oz.) noodles (2 cups)**
         in salted water for 7-8 minutes. Drain.
In a skillet melt:
         3 tbls. margarine
Add: **2 tbls. dry onion flakes**
         1/4 cup dry mushroom slices, broken
Combine and add:
         1 pkg. onion soup mix
         2 tbls. flour
Stir till smooth.
Add: **1 cup water, the rehydrated noodles and tvp**
Simmer 10 minutes, uncovered. Top with prepared sour cream mix, according to package directions.
3-4 servings

JAPANESE SPAGHETTI

At home, combine:
         1 pkg. tvp (1/2 cup) or dried cooked beef
         1 pkg. spaghetti sauce mix (check cooking times)
         1/4 cup tomato paste that has been "leathered"
Also take:
         2 bundles alimentary paste (Banshu Somen-it looks like
            white spaghetti)
At camp: To 3 cups water add tvp package. Simmer according to sauce package directions. Add broken "spaghetti" and simmer 3 minutes or according to directions. Add more water if needed.
   Variations: Substitute 1 can (8 oz.) minced clams for t.v.p. Include dry mushroom pieces.
2-3 servings

CHOW MEIN SUEY

At home, combine:
> **1 tbls. dry onion flakes**
> **1/2 cup dried celery slices**
> **1/2 cup dried bean sprouts**
> **1/4 cup dried sliced mushrooms**

Also include: **1 pkg. Proteinettes**

At camp: Boil and drain t.v.p. according to package directions. Rehydrate vegetables.

Combine:
> **2 tsp. beef bouillon**
> **1 tbls. cornstarch**
> **Salt and pepper**
> **1-1/2 cups water**

Add to rehydrated vegetables and t.v.p. Cook, stirring constantly till thickened and vegetables are tender. Serve over canned chow mein noodles.

3-4 servings

MEXICAN HASH

At home, combine:
> **1 pkg. t.v.p. (soak kind)**
> **1/3 cup dry onion flakes**
> **1/4 cup dry green pepper cubes**
> **1/2 cup dry tomato slices, broken**

Also take:
> **1/2 cup instant rice**
> **1 tsp. chili powder**

At camp: Rehydrate t.v.p. package. Return to heat, add water if needed. Simmer 7-10 minutes or till peppers are done. Drain, reserving liquid. Add water to make 1/2 cup. Add rice package and liquid. Simmer, covered, 5 minutes.

2 servings

MEXICAN SCRAMBLE

At home, combine:

2 pkg. t.v.p. (soak kind)
1 tbls. dry onion flakes
1 tbls. dry green pepper cubes
1/2 cup dry frozen corn
1/2 cup dry tomato slices
1/2 tsp. chili powder
1 tsp. salt

At camp: Rehydrate package (Check corn to see that is soft). Add 1 cup water. Bring to a boil, then simmer till vegetables are done. Add 1-1/3 cups instant rice. Cover and remove from heat. Let set 5-7 minutes, or till liquid is absorbed.

3-4 servings

CHILI 'N BEANS

At home, combine:

1 pkg. t.v.p. (soak kind)
1 cup cooked dried kidney beans
1 tbls. dry onion flakes
3/4 cup dried tomato slices, crushed
1/2 tsp. chili powder
1 tsp. salt, dash pepper

At camp: Rehydrate, then add 1 cup water and simmer 10-15 minutes. To thicken, add a package of brown gravy mix, stirring continually.

3-4 servings

QUICK CHILI

At home, combine:

1/4 cup dry onion flakes
2 pkgs. Lipton's Cup-a-Soup
1 large can kidney beans, drained and dried
1 tsp. chili powder
1 tsp. salt, dash of pepper

Also include: **1 pkg. Proteinettes (t.v.p.)**

At camp: Cook Proteinettes according to directions. Drain. Stir in other ingredients. Add water to barely cover. Bring to a boil, cover, remove from heat and let stand 10-15 minutes. Return to heat, and cook till beans are done.

3-4 servings

EGG FOO YOUNG

At home, combine:

1/4 cup dry onion flakes
1/2 cup dry celery slices
1/2 cup dry bean sprouts

Also take:

1 pkg. t.v.p. (soak kind)
1 cup dry egg powder

At camp: Rehydrate dry vegetables. Mix 1 cup egg powder with 1 cup water. Add t.v.p. and rehydrated vegetables. Fry by spoonfuls in a greased pan. Brown both sides. Serve with prepared beef or mushroom gravy mix.

Variation: Instead of t.v.p. use dry shrimp or dry chicken.

3-4 servings

Rice and Pasta

If rice has stuck (not burned) to the bottom of the pan, replace the cover and let set a few minutes off the heat. Most of the rice will be loosened.

RICE AS A SIDE DISH

Rice can be flavored in a variety of ways:
- Sauteed chopped celery and onion
- Chopped pimento
- Mushrooms and basil
- Tomatoes and chili powder
- Seasoning Mix (taco, sloppy joe, etc.)
- Curry, dill, parsley, grated citrus peel, garlic and onion salt
- Cinnamon, nutmeg, cinnamon sugar, mint
- Chopped dried fruit and raisins
- Juice crystals (orange, grapefruit, grape)
- Lemon crystals (to go with fresh trout)
- Crisp fried bacon or bacon bits
- Instant bouillon
- Shredded cheese or grated Parmesan cheese
- Nuts and seeds (almonds, sunflower, chia or poppy seeds)
- Dissolve fruit leather and combine with rice for dessert
- Saute rice and seasonings in margarine before adding water

CURRIED RICE

At home, combine:
> **1 cup instant rice**
> **1/4 tsp. dry garlic chips**
> **1 tsp. dry onion flakes**
> **2 tsp. instant chicken bouillon**
> **1 tsp. curry powder**
> **Dash of pepper**

At camp: Add 1 cup boiling water. Simmer 5 minutes, cover and remove from heat for 5 minutes.

2 servings

SPANISH RICE

At home, combine:
   1 tbls. dry onion flakes
   2 tbls. green pepper cubes
   2 tbls. dry celery slices
   2 tbls. dry tomato slices
   1/4 can tomato paste "leather"
Also take:
   1 cup instant rice
   1 tsp. chili powder
   Sharp cheddar cheese

At camp: Rehydrate vegetable package. Drain, reserving liquid. Add enough water to make 1 cup liquid. Combine vegetables, liquid and 1 cup instant rice. Bring to a boil, then simmer 5-7 minutes. Cut up cheese and stir into rice mixture till melted.

2 servings

ITALIAN RICE

At home, combine:
   1-1/3 cups instant rice
   1 tbls. dry onion flakes
   1/2 cup dry tomato slices
   2 tsp. instant chicken bouillon
   1-1/2 tsp. garlic salad dressing mix (or dry Italian
      seasoning mix)
Also take: **Grated Parmesan cheese**

At camp: In a pot, place 1-1/2 cups water, 2 tbls. margarine and the rice combination. Bring to a boil, then simmer 5-7 minutes. Remove from heat, cover and let set 5 minutes. Top each serving with cheese.

2 servings

CHINA RICE

At home, combine:
1/3 cup dry egg powder
2 tsp. dry onion flakes
1 tsp. each parsley and celery flakes
1/4 cup dry crumbled mushroom pieces
Also take:
1-1/2 cups instant rice
4 slices bacon or Canadian bacon (or 2 tsp. bacon bits)
At camp: Cut up bacon and fry till clear. Add rice and saute till browned. Add 1-1/2 cups water, bring to a boil, cover and let set 5 minutes off heat. Combine eggs with dry seasonings and 1/3 cup water. Add to rice and bacon. Return to heat and stir-cook till eggs are done.
2 servings

PASTA COOKING CHART

6-7 oz. macaroni (2 cups) = 4 cups cooked
7-8 oz. spaghetti = 4 cups cooked
8 oz. egg noodles (4-5 cups) = 4-5 cups cooked

EASY COOKING METHOD
(To save fuel)

Boil pasta in salted water, stirring constantly for 3 minutes. Cover tightly, remove from heat and let stand 10 minutes. Drain. Toss with margarine to keep pieces from sticking together. (Thicker pasta products like lasagne noodles should be cooked according to package directions.)

NOODLE FLAVORINGS

To melted margarine add:
Thyme, basil, parsley, onion or garlic chips
Grated Parmesan cheese
Cut-up processed cheese
Chia or poppy seeds
Toasted sunflower or pumpkin seeds

To make a complete meal, add rehydrated and cooked vegetables and meat of your choice to the cooked drained noodles.

Vegetable Dishes

CORN CURRY

At home, combine:
>   **1 pkg. dried frozen corn**
>   **1 tbls. green pepper cubes**
>   **1 tbls. dry onion flakes**
>   **1 tsp. curry powder**

Also take: **1 can (7 oz.) luncheon meat**

At camp: Rehydrate vegetables. Brown the cubed luncheon meat in margarine in a cooking pot. Add the vegetables and a little water if necessary. Simmer till vegetables are tender.

2 servings

SQUASH DISH

At home, combine:
>   **1 lb. (fresh weight) of any squash that has been dried**
>   **(zucchini, banana, etc.)**
>   **2 tbls. dry onion flakes**
>   **1/4 cup dry cooked ham**

At camp: Rehydrate squash package. Melt 2 tbls. margarine in a fry pan. Add squash, cover and simmer till tender, adding water if necessary. (Ham may need to be rinsed before rehydrating to remove excess salt.)

2 servings

SQUASH CASSEROLE

At home, combine:
>   **1 cup sliced, dried summer squash, broken up**
>   **1 cup dried tomato slices, broken**
>   **1 tbls. dry onion flakes**
>   **1/2 tsp. salt, dash pepper**

Also take: **1/2 cup croutons, plain or seasoned**

At camp: Rehydrate squash package, and then simmer till tender. Add croutons and stir to absorb excess moisture. Top each serving with a slice of cheese.

2-3 servings

ORIENTAL ASPARAGUS

At home, combine:

**1 cup dry frozen asparagus tips
1/2 cup dry mushroom pieces
Salt and pepper**

At camp: Rehydrate package. Add 2 tbls. margarine to a frying pan. Add vegetables and any liquid, and simmer covered, till tender. Top with bacon bits or crumbled dried ham or dry chicken.

2-3 servings

CABBAGE STEW

At home, combine:

**Dry shredded cabbage, carrots cut into thin circles,
celery cut into small pieces. (These can be prepared and
combined to dry together.)**

At camp: Add rinsed dry ham, caraway seed and dry onion flakes. Rehydrate, then simmer till done. Do not overcook.

(Amounts are variable)

CABBAGE HASH

At home, combine:

**Dry shredded cabbage (1 small head)
Dry tomato slices (1 large)
Dry celery slices (1 stalk)
Dry onion flakes (1 small onion)
Dry green chili peppers (2 peppers)**
Also take: **Ham cubes, dried, or bacon bits**

At camp: Rinse ham cubes. Add to vegetables and rehydrate. Simmer till vegetables are cooked.

NOODLES ITALIANO

Cook 1 pkg. Betty Crocker Noodles Italiano as directed on package.
Add: **2 tbls. margarine**
       1/4 cup dried mushrooms
       1/4 can tomato sauce, "leathered"
       1/4 cup water
Simmer 5 minutes. Add cheese packet and 1/4 cup water. Stir well,
and reheat.
   Variation: Add dried leafy vegetables or dry green beans for
more flavor. Top with bacon bits or crumbled dry ham cubes.
2-3 servings

MACARONI AND VEGETABLES

At home, combine:
       Macaroni from 1 pkg. macaroni and cheese dinner
       1 pkg. dried frozen green beans (Birdseye 5-minute)
       1 pkg. dried frozen corn
Also take:
       1/4 tsp. oregano
       1/4 tsp. chili powder
       Grated cheese from package
       1/4 cup dry milk
At camp: Boil macaroni and dried vegetables 7-10 minutes or till
vegetables are tender. Drain, reserving liquid. Add 1/3 cup of the
drained liquid and 2-3 tbls. margarine to the cheese package and
combine thoroughly. Add to the macaroni, stirring well. Simmer to
thicken.
3-4 servings

CHEESED VEGETABLES

At home, combine:
> **1 pkg. dried frozen corn (Birdseye 5-minute)**
> **2 small zucchini squash, sliced and dried**
> **2 tomatoes, sliced and dried**
> **1 tbls. dry onion flakes**
> **1/2 tsp. dry garlic chips**

At camp: Rehydrate vegetables. Simmer till corn is cooked. Top each serving with a generous slice of jack cheese.

2-3 servings

Chicken

CHICKEN JUMBLE

Combine:
> **3/4 cup cooked, cubed, dried chicken**
> **3/4 cup dried tomatoes, crushed**
> **1/4 cup dry celery slices**
> **1 tbls. dry onion flakes**
> **1 tbls. dry green pepper cubes**
> **1 tsp. salt, dash of pepper**

Also take: **1/2 cup instant rice**

At camp: Rehydrate chicken and vegetable package. Add 1 cup water and bring to a boil. Add rice, cover and simmer 2-3 minutes. Remove from heat for 5-7 minutes.

2-3 servings

FIESTA HOT POT

At home, combine:
> **1-1/2 cups cooked, cubed, dried chicken or turkey**
> **1/2 cup dried tomato slices, crushed**
> **1 pkg. Birdseye 5-minute corn, dried**
> **1/4 cup dry mushroom slices**

Also take: **1 pkg. chili seasoning mix**

At camp: Rehydrate chicken and vegetable package. Combine sauce mix and 1-1/2 cups water. (Include extra liquid from rehydrated vegetables.) Add rehydrated ingredients and simmer 15 minutes. Serve over crushed corn chips and top with shredded sharp cheddar cheese.

3-4 servings

RICE 'N CHICKEN

At home, combine:
>**1-1/3 cups instant rice**
>**2 tbls. dry onion flakes**
>**1/2 tsp. sage**
>**2 level tsp. instant bouillon**

At camp: Boil 1-2/3 cups water. Add dry ingredients and 1 can (5 oz.) boned chicken. (Or 1/2 cup cooked, cubed, dried chicken that has been rehydrated.) Simmer 5 minutes.

Variations: Add tuna instead of chicken. Add dry mushrooms.

2 servings

CHICKEN-NOODLE DINNER

At home, combine:
>**1/2 cup dried, cubed, cooked chicken**
>**1 tbls. dry onion flakes**
>**1/2 cup dried tomato slices, crushed**
>**1/4 cup each dried green beans and carrot slices**
>**1/2 cup crushed egg noodles**

Also take: **1 package chicken-noodle soup mix**

At camp: Bring four cups water to a boil. Add dry ingredients. Simmer till vegetables are cooked.

Variation: Add 1/4 cup grated Parmesan cheese just before serving.

2-3 servings

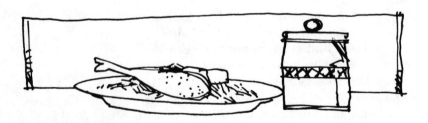

CHICKEN 'N DUMPLINGS

At home, combine:
> **1/2 cup cooked, cubed, dried chicken**
> **2 tsp. dry onion flakes**
> **1/2 tsp. each dry parsley and celery leaves**
> **Dash of pepper**
> **2 tsp. instant chicken bouillon**
> **1/4 cup each dry carrot slices and dry peas**

In another plastic bag, combine:
> **1 cup flour**
> **2 tsp. baking powder**
> **1/2 tsp. salt**
> **1/3 cup dry milk**

At camp: Rehydrate dry chicken and vegetable package. Add more water to cover about 1/2" and bring to a boil. Combine flour package with 1/2 cup water. Mix into a thick batter and drop by spoonfuls into boiling chicken mixture. Cover tightly, reduce heat and cook 20 minutes without raising the lid.

3-4 servings

To Betty Crocker Noodles Almondine mix, add:
> Rehydrated chicken or tuna
> Rehydrated pineapple slices, cubed
> Rehydrated green pepper cubes
> Rehydrated mushroom pieces
> Rehydrated carrots, green beans, or peas

DINNER FOR TWO

At home, combine:
> **1 cooked, cubed, dried chicken breast**
> **1 pkg. frozen peas and carrots, dried**
> **1/4 tsp. marjoram**

Also take: **1 pkg. chicken gravy mix**

At camp: Rehydrate chicken and vegetables. Add 3/4 cup water and bring to a boil. Simmer till carrots are tender. Add gravy mix, stirring constantly till smooth and thickened. Serve over Mrs. Reis No-Cook Noodles.

2 servings

CHICKEN A'LA KING

At home, combine:
> **1 cup cooked, cubed, dried chicken**
> **1/2 cup dried asparagus tips**
> **1/2 cup dried mushroom pieces**
> **1/4 cup dried celery slices**
> **2 tbls. dried sweet red pepper cubes**
> **1/2 tsp. salt, dash of pepper**

In another bag, combine:
> **1 tbls. flour**
> **2/3 cup dry milk**
> **2 tbls. dry egg powder**
> **1/4 tsp. salt, dash of pepper**
> **1/2 tsp. paprika**

At camp: Rehydrate chicken and vegetables, then cook till celery is tender. Add two cups water to the bag containing the flour mixture. Combine well, then pour slowly over boiling chicken, stirring constantly till thickened. Serve over toasted bread or shredded wheat biscuits.

Variation: Use dry broccoli instead of asparagus.

4 servings

CREAMED CHICKEN AND CHEESE

At home, combine:
> **1/2 cup cooked, cubed, dried chicken**
> **1/4 cup dried mushroom pieces**

Also combine, separately:
> **1 tbls. flour**
> **2 tbls. dry milk**
> **Salt and pepper**

At camp: Rehydrate dried chicken and mushrooms. Add 1 tbls. margarine and simmer till chicken is soft. Add more water if necessary. Moisten flour mixture with 1/4 cup water, stir into chicken and cook till thickened. Add 1/4 cup shredded Jack cheese and stir till melted. Serve over flavored croutons.

2 servings

QUICK CREAMED CHICKEN

At home, combine:

3 pkgs. Lipton's Mushroom Cup-a-Soup
1/2 cup dried frozen peas
1/2 cup dried, cooked, cubed chicken

Also take: **1/2 cup instant potato flakes, separately.**

At camp: Bring 4 cups water to a boil. Add dry chicken package. Rehydrate 10-15 minutes. Return to a simmer and add potato flakes to thicken.

3 servings

CHICKEN AND GREENS

At home, combine:

Approx. 2 dozen dried leaves of chard, spinach, beets or
Romaine lettuce, or a combination
1/2 cup dry tomato slices
1 tsp. dry onion flakes
1/2 tsp. garlic salt
1/2 tsp. oregano
1/2 to 3/4 cup dry chicken cubes that have been crumbled
in a blender

Also take: **1-1/3 cups instant rice**

At camp: Rehydrate dry vegetable and chicken package. Simmer till chicken is soft. Drain remaining liquid into a cup and add water to make 1-1/3 cups liquid. Return to pot. Bring to a boil. Add 1 tbls. margarine and rice. Cover and set off heat 5-7 minutes.

2-3 servings

POLYNESIAN CHICKEN

At home, marinate cooked, cubed chicken several hours or overnight in:
> **Marinade: 2 tbls. soy sauce**
> **2 tbls. orange juice**
> **1 tsp. brown sugar**
> **1/4 tsp. dry garlic chips**
> **1/4 tsp. powdered ginger**

Drain and dry according to directions.

At camp, combine dried marinated chicken with dry asparagus tips. Rehydrate, then simmer till cooked. (Use approximately 1 chicken breast and 1/2 cup dry asparagus.)

2 servings.

ORIENTAL SPAGHETTI

At home, combine:
> **1 cup dried, cooked, cubed chicken**
> **2 tbls. dried cubed green pepper**
> **2 tbls. dried sliced celery**
> **2 tbls. dry onion flakes**
> **1/2 tsp. dry garlic chips**
> **1 tsp. dry parsley flakes**
> **1/2 can dried (leathered) tomato paste**

Also take: **Approx. 8 oz. Oriental Banshu Somen (looks like white spaghetti)**
> **Grated Parmesan cheese**

At camp: Rehydrate meat and vegetables; simmer till soft. Add approximately 2 cups water, bring to a boil. Add broken alimentary paste and simmer 3 minutes or till water is absorbed. Top with Parmesan cheese.

4-5 servings

Ham Dishes

HAWAIIAN RICE

At home, package:
> **1 can (7 oz.) Spam**
> **1-1/3 cups instant rice**
> **1/3-1/2 cup flaked coconut**

At camp: Melt 1 tbls. margarine in a frying pan. Add cubed Spam and rice and brown slightly. Add 1-1/3 cups water and bring to a boil. Cover and remove from heat for 5 minutes. Add coconut and toss to mix.

2 servings

HAM-VEGETABLE POT

At home, combine:
> **1 pkg. Birdseye 5-minute frozen corn, dried**
> **1 pkg. Birdseye 5-minute frozen lima beans, dried**
> **1/4 cup dried mushroom pieces**

Also take: **1/2 cup dried ham cubes (to be rinsed in hot water at camp)**

Also take:
> **Sauce Mix: 3/4 cup dry milk**
> **3 tbls. flour**
> **1/2 tsp. onion powder**
> **1/4 tsp. sage**
> **1/2 tsp. celery seed**

At camp: Rehydrate vegetables and ham, and simmer till soft. Combine sauce mix with 1-1/2 cups water. Add to simmering vegetables, stirring constantly. Serve over chow mein noodles.

2-3 servings

ORIENTAL STROGANOFF

At home, combine:

1/2 cup dried ham cubes
2 tbls. dry minced onion
1/3 cup dried mushroom pieces
1 pkg. (10 oz.) frozen mixed vegetables, dried
1/2 cup dried tomato slices, broken

Also take:

1 cup instant rice
1/4 tsp. oregano

At camp: Rehydrate ham and vegetables. Return to heat and simmer till vegetables are done. Add rice package, 1 cup water. Bring to a boil, cover, and simmer 5 minutes. Top with sour cream prepared from a package.

2-3 servings

Pork

CHINESE PORK AND RICE

At home, combine:

1 tbls. dry onion flakes
1 tbls. dry green pepper cubes
1/2 cup dry celery slices
1 cup pork that has been cooked, cubed and dried

Also take:

1 cup instant rice
1 tsp. instant chicken bouillon

At camp: Rehydrate vegetables and pork, then simmer till celery is cooked. Drain extra liquid into a cup and add enough water to make 1 cup. Add rice package and 1 tbls. margarine. Reheat, cover and remove from heat for 5-7 minutes.

2-3 servings

HONG KONG DINNER

At home, combine:

1/2 cup pork that has been cooked, cubed and dried
1/2 cup pineapple pieces, dried (canned or fresh)
1/2 cup green pepper, cubed and dried
1 tbls. onion flakes, dried

Also take: **1-1/2 cups instant rice**

At camp: Rehydrate pork package, then simmer a few minutes till tender. Drain remaining liquid into a cup. Add water to make 1-1/2 cups. Return liquid to pot. Bring to a boil, add rice and salt and pepper to taste. Stir well, cover, and remove from heat 5-7 minutes.

2-3 servings

Beef

BEEF AND CARROT STEW

At home, combine:

1 tsp. instant minced onion
1 tsp. instant beef bouillon
1/2 cup carrot slices, dried
1/4 cup celery slices, dried
1/2 cup dried cooked beef slices (lean) broken up

At camp: Rehydrate in 1-1/2 cups water. Then simmer till celery and carrots are crisp cooked.

Variation: Substitute or add green beans (dried) or dried chard.

2 servings

BEEF STEW FOR A CROWD

At home, combine:

Dry sliced carrots
Dry sliced potatoes from a potato casserole mix
Dry green beans (Birdseye frozen 5-minute vegetable)
Dry shredded cabbage
Dry green pepper cubes
Dry tomato slices
Dry slices of lean cooked beef

Also take: **1 envelope dry onion soup mix mixed with 2 tbls. flour.**

At camp: Rehydrate dry vegetables and meat. Simmer till carrots are nearly cooked. Add onion soup mix with flour and simmer 5 minutes more.

WILDERNESS KASHA

At home, combine:
2 cups kasha (in Jewish section of market)
1 tsp. salt
1 tbls. dry onion flakes
Jerky which has been dried without seasoning
1 pkg. au jus gravy mix

At camp: Heat 4 cups water to boiling. Add 2-3 tbls. margarine and dry ingredients. Cook according to kasha package directions.

Chipped Beef and Salami

GRILLED SANDWICH FILLING

Combine:
1 can (8 oz.) tomato sauce that has been "leathered"
1 cup shredded cheese (Jack or cheddar)
1 cup finely chopped dry salami
1/2 tsp. oregano
1/4 tsp. garlic powder

At camp: Add just enough water to make a thick paste. Spread margarine on two slices of rye or French bread (for one sandwich). Place filling on one unspread side and place buttered-side down in a hot skillet. Top with the other slice of bread, spread side up. Brown both sides.

CREAMED CHIPPED BEEF

At home, combine:
1/3 cup dry milk
1/3 cup coffee lightener (Preem)
2 tbls. flour

Also include: **1 jar or package of dried chipped beef**

At camp: Add 1 cup water to dry milk mixture and stir till well blended. Add chipped beef which has been rinsed, drained and shredded. Simmer till mixture is thickened. Serve over toast, canned Chinese noodles or shredded wheat biscuit.

2 servings

MACARONI 'N BEEF

At home, combine:

1 pkg. Golden Grain Mushroom Soup mix
1/4 lb. dried chipped beef, shredded

Also take: **1 pkg. macaroni and cheese (Kraft, Betty Crocker, etc.)**

At camp: Cook macaroni as directed on package for skillet method. Drain. Blend in 1-1/2 cups water, soup mix, cheese sauce mix and dried beef. Bring to a boil and simmer a few minutes. Add more water if necessary.

Variation: Add dried green vegetables or greens.

2-3 servings

DRIED BEEF AND PASTA

At home, combine:

2 pkgs. Lipton Mushroom Cup-a-Soup
1/2 cup dry milk
1 tbls. dry onion flakes
2 tbls. dry egg powder

Also include:

1 cup elbow macaroni
1 4-5 oz. pkg. wafer-sliced dried beef

At camp: Bring 3 cups water to a rapid boil. Rinse dried beef in this water to remove salt. Drain beef on a paper towel, and add macaroni to the same water. Boil rapidly for three minutes. Cover tightly, remove from heat and let stand 10 minutes (to save fuel). Drain and toss with 1 tbls. margarine. Combine soup package with 2 cups water. Add to macaroni along with dried beef. Reheat to simmering and cook approximately 10 minutes. Top each serving with shredded cheese if desired.

2-3 servings

CABBAGE CASSEROLE

At home, combine:

1 cup shredded dried cabbage
1 cup dried apple slices, broken into small pieces
1/4 tsp. caraway seeds
Salt and pepper

Also take: **6-8 dry salami slices cut into quarters.**

At camp: Rehydrate the dry ingredients, then simmer briefly. Add cut-up salami and reheat if necessary.

2-3 servings

SALAMI SCALLOP

At home, combine:

1/4 cup dried green pepper cubes
1/4 cup dry onion flakes
2 cups dry zucchini slices

Also take:

6-8 slices of dry salami

At camp: In a fry pan, frizzle the cut-up, thin-sliced salami. Rehydrate the vegetables, then add with the remaining liquid. Simmer till green pepper is cooked. (Thicken with a little potato flakes, if desired.) Serve over crushed cheese crackers.

2 servings

COMBO BEANS

At home, combine:

1 cup cooked pinto beans, dried
1/4 cup garbanzo beans, cooked and dried
1/4 cup green beans, cooked and dried
1/4 cup lima beans, cooked and dried
2 tsp. dry onion flakes
1/4 tsp. celery seed

(For convenience, dry canned beans which have been well drained.)

Also take: **Approximately 12 oz. dry salami slices**

At camp: Rehydrate the beans and onion. In a frying pan, fry the salami slices till the edges curl. Add the beans and enough liquid to barely cover. Simmer till the beans are soft. Season to taste.

2 servings

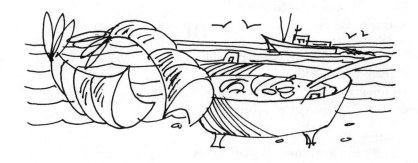

Seafood

CLAM CHOWDER

At home, combine:

2 tsp. Wilson's Bits 'O Bacon
1/4 cup dry sliced carrots
1/4 cup dry sliced celery
1/4 cup dry cubed green pepper

Also take:

1/2 cup dry milk
1/4 cup coffee lightener

And include:

2 cans (6 oz. each) minced clams
1 pkg. Wyler's Potato Soup with Leek

At camp: Rehydrate dry vegetables. Return to heat, and add 4 cups water. Bring to a boil. Add potato soup and simmer till vegetables are cooked. Add clams and juice and the dry milk package. Reheat, but DO NOT BOIL.

2-3 servings

CLAM FRITTERS

At home, combine:
> **2 cups flour**
> **1-1/2 tsp. baking powder**
> **1 tsp. salt**
> **1/2 cup dry milk**
> **2 heaping tbls. dry egg powder (or 1 fresh egg)**

Also take: **1 can minced clams.**

At camp: Drain clam liquid into a cup and add water to make 1 cup liquid (approximate). Combine liquid and dry ingredients. Fold in minced clams. Drop by tablespoons onto a hot greased frying pan. Brown both sides.

3-4 servings

SHRIMP CREOLE

At home, combine:
> **1 cup dry summer squash slices**
> **1 tbls. dry onion flakes**
> **1/2 cup dry tomato slices**
> **1 tsp. dry parsley**
> **1/4 tsp. celery salt**
> **Dash of pepper**

In a separate bag, include: **3/4 cup dry shrimp**

At camp: Rehydrate all ingredients together. Add a dollop of margarine, and return to heat. Add water if necessary and cook till ingredients are tender.

2 servings

SHRIMP PATTIES

At home, combine:
> **1/3 cup dry egg powder**
> **2 tbls. flour**
> **1/4 tsp. salt, dash of pepper**

Also take: **1/4 cup dried shrimp**

At camp: Rehydrate the shrimp. Add shrimp and remaining liquid to the dry ingredients. Add more water if necessary to make a thick batter. Fry by spoonfuls on a hot greased frying pan, turning brown brown both sides.

SHRIMP CAKES

At home, combine:
> **1/2 cup dried shrimp**
> **1/3 cup dry egg powder**
> **1 tbls. dry onion flakes**
> **2 tbls. crumbled dry mushroom slices**
> **Salt and pepper**

Also take: **4-5 servings of instant mashed potato flakes**

At camp: Add water to barely cover the shrimp combination. Rehydrate. Add mashed potato flakes and enough water to moisten. Mix well. Melt 1 tbls. margarine in a skillet. Drop shrimp mixture by spoonfulls into hot frying pan. Flatten with a spatula. Brown each side, adding more margarine when necessary.

Variation: Prepare a package of onion gravy mix to serve over cakes.

3-4 servings

SHRIMP STEW

At home, combine:
> **1/2 cup dried celery slices**
> **1/4 cup dried mushroom pieces**

Also take:
> **1 tbls. cornstarch**
> **1 tsp. instant chicken bouillon**

Add: **1 can (4-1/2 oz.) shrimp**

At camp: Rehydrate celery and mushroom, then simmer till celery is cooked. Combine cornstarch, bouillon and 2 tbls. cold water. Add 1 cup water. Rinse and drain shrimp. Simmer all together 5-7 minutes. Serve over canned Chinese noodles, prepared instant rice, or croutons.

2-3 servings

CREAMED SHRIMP

At home, combine:
>1 tsp. dry onion flakes
>1 tsp. dry parsley flakes
>1/4 cup flour
>1/2 cup dry milk
>1 tsp. salt
>1/2 tsp. chili powder

Also pack:
>2 cans (5-3/4 oz. each) water-packed shrimp (or the equivalent, dried, then rehydrated at camp)
>2-3 individual packets of catsup

At camp: Add 2 cups water to the dry ingredients and stir till smooth. Cook 5 minutes, stirring constantly. Add shrimp (drained) and catsup. Heat till bubbly.

3-4 servings

SHRIMP CHOWDER

At home, combine:
>2 tsp. Wilson's Bits 'O Bacon
>1 tbls. dry green pepper cubes
>1 tbls. dry onion flakes
>3/4 cup dry milk

Package separately:
>3/4 cup dry shrimp
>1/2 cup instant mashed potato

At camp: Bring 2 cups water to a boil. Add dry ingredients and simmer till pepper flakes are soft.

>*Variation:* Add 1/2 cup shredded Jack cheese and stir till melted.

2 servings

MEXICAN "DRY SOUP"

At home, combine:
   1 tbls. dry onion flakes
   1/2 tsp. dry garlic chips
   1 tsp. dry parsley flakes
   1/2 cup dried tomatoes, crushed
   2 heaping tsp. chicken bouillon
   **2 dried, broken green chili peppers (see how to prepare
      in chapter on drying)**
Also package separately:
   1/2-3/4 cup dried cooked shrimp
Also take: **1 cup instant rice**

At camp: Rehydrate vegetables and shrimp, then simmer 5 minutes. Drain any remaining liquid into a cup and add water to make one cup. In a pot: Heat 2-3 tbls. margarine. Add rice and brown lightly. Slowly add liquid and vegetables and shrimp. Cover and simmer 5-10 minutes. Add more water if necessary.

   Variations: Add ham-flavored Proteinettes instead of shrimp. Add rehydrated peas or corn.

3 generous servings

SALMON ROMANOFF

Prepare 1 package Noodles Romanoff as directed on the package, except use 2/3 cup milk. Drain and flake 1 can (7-3/4 oz.) salmon, and add to noodles. Cover and simmer 12-15 minutes.

   Variation: Use any canned seafood of your choice.

2 servings

OYSTER STEW

At home, combine:
   1-1/3 cups dry milk
   1 tsp. salt, dash of pepper
   1 tsp. celery salt
Also take: **1 can (6-1/2 oz.) oysters**

At camp: Combine oysters, liquor, and 1 tbls. margarine in a pot. Simmer for 5 minutes. Add 4 cups water and the dry ingredients and heat just to a simmer. DO NOT BOIL. (Add 1/3 cup coffee lightener for more "body.")

2-3 servings

TUNA MUFFINS

At home, combine:
> **1/2 cup dried tuna**
> **1/2 cup dried, crumbled tomato slices**
> **1/4 tsp. dry garlic chips**
> **1 tbls. dry onion flakes**

Also take:
> **8 Swiss cheese slices**
> **3 tbls. grated Parmesan cheese**
> **4 English muffins, split**

At camp: Rehydrate dry ingredients. Return to heat and simmer till liquid is mostly evaporated. Place buttered English muffins, cut-side up in a frying pan, top with tuna mixture, Swiss cheese slice and parmesan. Cover and warm over low flame till cheese melts.

8 servings

TUNA SKILLET DINNER

At home, combine:
> **1/2 cup dried water-packed tuna**
> **1/2 cup dried frozen peas**
> **2 heaping tsp. instant chicken bouillon**

Also take: **1 cup instant rice**

At camp: Rehydrate tuna package. Bring to a boil, and simmer till peas are tender. Drain remaining liquid into a cup and add water to measure 1 cup. Return to pot and add rice. Add salt and pepper and bring to a boil. Cover and simmer 5 minutes.

2-3 servings

CREAMED TUNA POT

At home, combine:
>**1/2 cup dried water-packed tuna**
>**1 pkg. Birdseye 5-minute frozen peas, dried**
>**1 pkg. Birdseye 5-minute frozen asparagus tips, dried**

Also combine:
>**3 tbls. flour**
>**1/4 tsp. dill weed**
>**3/4 cup dry milk**
>**3/4 tsp. salt, dash of pepper**

At camp: Rehydrate dry tuna package, then simmer 5 minutes. Combine flour package with 1-1/2 cups water (part vegetable liquid) and add to tuna. Stir and simmer till sauce thickens. Cook for 5 minutes. Serve over croutons.

2-3 servings

TUNA CHOW MEIN

At home, combine:
>**1/2 cup dry celery slices**
>**1 tbls. dry onion flakes**
>**2 tbls. dry green pepper cubes**
>**1/4 cup dry mushroom pieces**

Also take:
>**2 tbls. dry milk**
>**1 tbls. flour**
>**2 tbls. instant chicken bouillon**

Include: **1 can tuna (or the dried equivalent)**

At camp: Rehydrate celery package, and simmer till celery is cooked. Drain liquid into a cup and add water to make 1/2 cup liquid. Stir into flour mixture to make a smooth paste. Add to vegetables along with 2 tbls. margarine. Add tuna, drained. Stir and cook till thickened. Serve over canned chow mein noodles.

3-4 servings

TUNA STRAWS

At home, combine:
> **1 pkg. cream of mushroom soup (Knorr's, Lipton's)**
> **2/3 cup dry milk**
> **1/4 cup dry mushroom pieces**

Also take:
> **1 can tuna**
> **1 can (4 oz.) shoestring potatoes transferred to a**
>   **plastic bag**

At camp: Combine dry ingredients with the tuna and the water required for the soup directions. When heated and the mushrooms are soft, pour over the shoestring potatoes. (If the mixture is too thin, thicken with a little quick-cook cereal or pancake mix moistened with a little water.)

2-3 servings

TUNA CURRY

At home, combine:
> **1 pkg. sour cream sauce mix**
> **1/3 cup dry milk**
> **1 tsp. dry onion flakes**
> **1 tsp. curry powder**

Also take: **1 can tuna (or 1 can dried water-packed tuna).**

At camp: Combine 2/3 cup water with sour cream mix. Let stand 10 minutes. Heat tuna and a little water in a saucepan (or use rehydrated tuna). Add sour cream combination and reheat, but DO NOT BOIL. Serve over crushed Chinese noodles.

2-3 servings

TUNA CASSEROLE

At home, combine:
> **1 pkg. vegetable soup mix (Wyler's)**
> **2 packets Lipton's Tomato Cup-a-Soup**
> **1 can water-packed tuna that has been dried**

Also take: **1 cup instant rice**

At camp: Bring 2-1/2 cups water to a boil. Add dry ingredients. Simmer 8-10 minutes. Add rice, cover, and remove from heat for 5 minutes.

2-3 servings

Casseroles to Dry

The following recipes are to be cooked and dried at home, then packaged before the start of the trip. At camp, rehydration is all that is necessary.

When preparing ground meat casseroles, be sure to drain the fat from browned hamburger, then spread it out on paper towels and blot to eliminate as much grease as possible. Fat becomes rancid very quickly.

When drying a casserole dish, spread it out very loosely. DO NOT CROWD. The ingredients will sour and spoil if the drying process takes too long.

Cool the cooked casserole for an hour, then spread the ingredients on plastic wrap to begin drying. Stir occasionally. Finish drying on cheesecloth, nylon net or paper towels.

SPAGHETTI-CHICKEN CASSEROLE

Prepare and dry at home:

> **1 8 oz. pkg. spaghetti**
> **1 onion, chopped**
> **1 small clove garlic, pressed**
> **1 cup mushroom slices**
> **2 tbls. margarine**
> **2-1/2 cups (1 large can) cooked tomatoes**
> **1 tbls. sugar**
> **1 cup (or more) cooked chicken**
> **Salt and pepper to taste**

Cook spaghetti according to package directions. Drain. Saute onion, garlic and mushrooms in margarine till tender. Add the rest of the ingredients and heat to boiling. Stir in drained spaghetti and mix well. Turn into greased 2-quart casserole and bake at 350° for 45 minutes. Cool for an hour, then spread the ingredients on plastic wrap very loosely and dry. Stir occasionally. Finish the drying process on cheesecloth, nylon net, or paper towels.

3-4 servings

MACARONI ITALIANO

Prepare and dry at home:

Boil 2 cups macaroni in salted water according to package directions. Drain.

Combine in a blender:

1 can (1 lb.) stewed tomatoes plus water to make 2 cups
1 large stalk celery, cut up
1/2 of a cleaned green pepper
2-3 sprigs fresh parsley
1/2 of a small onion

Put blender ingredients into a saucepan with:

1/2 can ripe olives, sliced
1/2 tsp. oregano
1 tsp. sugar
1 tsp. Worcestershire sauce
1 tsp. salt, dash of pepper

Heat to boiling. Add cooked macaroni, mix well, and pour into a greased 2-quart casserole. Sprinkle generously with Parmesan cheese. Bake at 350° for 45-50 minutes. Cool and dry according to directions.

Variations: Spanish Macaroni: Use tomato sauce and water for liquid instead of canned tomatoes. Add 1 XLNT Tamale, cut up. Use basil instead of oregano.

3-4 servings

FIESTA RICE

Prepare and dry at home:

Saute 1-1/2 pounds ground beef till the meat is well browned. Drain thoroughly and spread on paper towels. Blot as much fat as possible. Return to frying pan that has been wiped out with a paper towel.

Add: **1 large onion, chopped**
1 tsp. salt
1 cup uncooked rice
4 cups tomato juice, heated

Bring to a boil. Pour into a greased 2-quart casserole and bake at 350° for 35-40 minutes or till liquid is absorbed. Cool and dry according to directions. When packaging, try adding some bacon bits for a change of flavor at camp.

3-4 servings

SPANISH RICE

Prepare and dry at home:
> **1 tbls. margarine**
> **3/4 cup uncooked rice**
> **1/2 cup chopped onion**
> **1/2 cup chopped green pepper**
> **1/2 cup diced celery**
> **2 cans (1 lb. each) whole tomatoes**
> **1 cup water**
> **1-1/2 tsp. salt, dash of pepper**
> **1 tsp. sugar**
> **1/2 tsp. chili powder**

In a heavy skillet, brown the rice in the margarine till golden. Add onion, green pepper and celery and stir-fry 2-3 minutes. Add other ingredients, cover and cook over low heat till rice is tender (up to an hour). Stir occasionally. Cool and dry according to directions.

At camp, top each serving with a generous slice of cheese.

3-4 servings

BEAN CASSEROLE

Prepare and dry at home:
> **2 tbls. margarine**
> **1 large onion, chopped**
> **1 cup snipped dried apricots (or any dried fruit)**
> **2 cans Boston baked beans**
> **3 tbls. firmly packed brown sugar**
> **1 tbls. dry mustard**
> **1 tsp. salt, dash of pepper**
> **Dry salami (to be added at camp)**

In a 4-quart kettle: Saute the onion in the margarine until limp. Add apricots, beans, brown sugar, mustard, salt and pepper, and heat to boiling. Place in a greased 2-quart casserole, cover and bake at 350° for 45 minutes. Cool and dry according to directions.

At camp: Top each serving with slivers of dry salami

4-5 servings

MULTI-BEAN POT

Prepare and dry at home:
1 lb. ground beef
1 can (1 lb.) stewed or plain whole tomatoes
1 can (1 lb.) Boston baked beans
1 can (1 lb.) kidney beans
1 can (1 lb.) lima beans
1 pkg. chili mix
1/4 cup packed brown sugar

Brown ground beef and drain thoroughly on paper towels. Return to pan. Add remaining ingredients and slow-simmer, uncovered, for 1/2 hour to evaporate as much excess liquid as possible. Cool and dry according to directions.

5-6 servings

BASIC BEAN SOUP

Prepare and dry at home:

In a 3-quart kettle: Brown 1 cup very lean ham scraps. Add beans that have been soaked overnight or prepared according to package directions. Use 2 cups dry navy, pinto, kidney, garbanzos, blackeye peas, or limas.
Also add:
1 can (1 lb. 12 oz.) whole tomatoes, cut up
1 can (8 oz.) tomato sauce
2 large celery stalks, cut into 1/2-inch pieces
1 large onion, chopped
1 large garlic clove, pressed
1 tsp. sugar (to cut tomato sharpness)
Water to barely cover beans

Simmer, covered, 2-3 hours or till beans are tender. Partially uncover and allow liquid to evaporate and contents to thicken.
Add: **Salt and pepper to taste**
1/2 tsp. marjoram
1 tsp. chili powder (optional)
Simmer 10 minutes more. Cool and dry according to directions.

4-5 servings

GARBANZO "DRY" SOUP

Prepare and dry at home:

Wash, then simmer 2 cups garbanzo dry beans in water to cover till tender, 1 hour to 2 hours.

Add: **Left-over lean meat scraps (beef, ham or chicken)**
2 stalks celery, cut into small pieces. Include a few leaves
1 small onion, chopped
1 can (1 lb. 12 oz.) whole tomatoes and juice
1 clove garlic, pressed
1/2 tsp. marjoram
1 tsp. salt, dash of pepper
1 tsp. sugar

Add only enough water to cook with. Simmer, covered, approximately 1 hour or till garbanzos are soft. Cool, then whirl in a blender a cup at a time. Spread on plastic wrap to dry as you would leather.

At camp: Drop pieces into hot bouillon and stir to dissolve.

Variation: For a "hot" flavor, add a 7 oz. can of diced green chilis.

4-5 servings

BEEF FIESTA

Prepare and dry at home:
Combine:

1 lb. ground beef that has been browned and drained
1/4 cup diced onion
1 can (1 lb.) tomatoes, cut up
1 can (12 oz.) whole kernel corn
1/2 cup green pepper cubes
1 tsp. salt, dash of pepper
1 tsp. chili powder
2 tsp. instant beef bouillon
1-1/4 cups water

Bring to a boil, then simmer 15-20 minutes. Add 1-1/3 cups instant rice. Remove from heat, cover, and let set 5-7 minutes. Cool and dry according to directions.

3-4 servings

MEXICAN HASH

Prepare and dry at home:
Combine:

1 lb. ground beef that has been browned and drained
2 large onions, sliced
1 green pepper, chopped
1 large stalk celery, cut into small pieces
1 can (1 lb.) stewed tomatoes
1 can (1 lb.) whole kernel corn, drained
1/2 cup uncooked regular rice
1 tsp. chili powder
2 tsp. salt, dash of pepper
2 cans (4 oz. each) diced green chilis

Heat, then pour into a greased 2-quart casserole. Bake, covered, at 350° for 1 hour. Remove cover and and bake 10 minutes more. Cool and dry according to directions.

Chef's Secret—Chocolate takes the "fire" out of hot Mexican food. Serve hot chocolate with Mexican Hash.

3-4 servings

HONEYED CHICKEN

Prepare and dry at home:
In a 2-quart greased casserole, combine:

2 cups cooked, cut-up chicken
1/2 tsp. curry powder
1/4 cup honey
1 tbls. prepared mustard

Stir until the chicken is well coated.
Add: **1-1/2 cups water**
1 heaping tsp. instant chicken bouillon
1/4 cup chopped onion
1/2 cup snipped dried fruit (apple, prune, pineapple)
1-1/3 cups instant rice

Bake at 350° for 25-30 minutes, covered. Remove cover and bake a few minutes more to evaporate extra liquid. Cool and dry according to directions.

At camp: Top each serving with toasted sunflower seeds.

3-4 servings

TROPICAL CHICKEN

Prepare and dry at home:
Combine:
> **2 cups cooked cubed chicken**
> **1 can (9 oz.) frozen orange juice concentrate**
> **1 can (9 oz.) crushed pineapple**
> **1 tbls. soy sauce**
> **1 tsp. ginger**
> **1-1/3 cups instant rice**
> **1/2 tsp. salt, dash of pepper**

Pour into a greased 2-quart casserole and bake, covered, 25-30 minutes. Cool and dry according to directions.

3-4 servings

TANGY CHICKEN

Prepare and dry at home:
Saute: **1/4 cup margarine**
> **1-2/3 cups thinly sliced carrots**
> **1/4 cup chopped onion**

Cook until onion is limp and carrots are almost tender.
Add: **1 cup fresh orange juice**
> **1 cup water**
> **2 tbls. brown sugar**
> **1 tsp. salt, dash of pepper**
> **1 tsp. grated orange rind**
> **1/2 tsp. poultry seasoning**

Bring to a boil.
Add: **1-1/2 cups cooked cubed chicken**
> **1-1/3 cups instant rice**

Cover and simmer 8-10 minutes. Remove cover and continue cooking while stirring to eliminate as much liquid as possible. Cool and dry according to directions.

3-4 servings

HAM CASSEROLE

Prepare and dry at home:
Combine in a 2-quart casserole:

> **1-1/2 cups cooked lean ham, cut into 1/2" cubes**
> **1/2 cup chopped onion**
> **1 cup peeled, diced, tart apples**
> **1/2 cup chopped dry prunes**
> **1/2 cup diced orange sections**
> **1-1/3 cups instant rice**
> **1-1/2 tsp. salt, dash of pepper**
> **1/8 tsp. poultry seasoning**
> **1-1/3 cups hot water**

Cover and bake at 350° for 45-55 minutes. Cool and dry according to directions.

3-4 servings

BLACK-EYED PEAS AND HAM

Prepare and dry at home:
Combine and saute:

> **2 tbls. margarine**
> **1/2 cup cooked cubed ham, very lean**
> **1/4 cup chopped onion**
> **1/4 cup chopped celery**

When celery is partially cooked, add:

> **1 can (1 lb.) black-eyed peas and liquid**

Cover and simmer 5 minutes.

Add: **1 scant cup water**
> **1 cup instant rice**

Bring to a boil, cover, and simmer 5 minutes, or till liquid is absorbed. Cool and dry according to directions.

2-3 servings

HAM CALIFORNIAN

Prepare and dry at home:
Combine:

        1 cup cooked, cubed, lean ham
        1/2 cup diced celery
        1 can mushroom pieces, drained
        1-1/2 cups water
        1 can (1 lb.) stewed tomatoes
        1 pkg. onion soup mix
        1-1/3 cups instant rice

Pour into a 2-quart greased casserole. Cover and bake at 375° for 45 minutes. Cool and dry according to directions.

    At camp: Top each serving with sharp cheddar cheese.

2-3 servings

TUNA DELIGHT

Prepare and dry at home:
Combine in a 4-quart saucepan:

      1 can (7 oz.) water-packed tuna, drained
      2 tbls. chopped onion
      1 small can mushroom pieces, drained
      1 cup thin-sliced carrots
      1 can (1 lb.) peas and juice
      1-1/3 cups instant rice
      1 cup hot water
      1/2 tsp. salt, dash of pepper
      1/2 tsp. Worcestershire sauce
      2 tsp. lemon juice

Bring to a boil, cover and cook over low heat about 10 minutes or until liquid is absorbed. Cool and dry according to directions.

2-3 servings

CRAB CASSEROLE

Prepare and dry at home:
In a 3-quart saucepan, combine:

      1 pkg. (9 oz.) frozen green beans
      1 can (1 lb.) stewed tomatoes, cut up
      1 can (7 oz.) crab meat, drained
      3/4 cup water
      2 tbls. margarine
      1/2 tsp. sugar
      1 tsp. dry celery leaves
      1 tsp. dry parsley leaves
      3/4 cup instant rice
      1/2 tsp. salt, dash of pepper

Heat till bubbly. Pour into a greased 2-quart casserole. Cover and bake at 400° for 25-30 minutes. Cool and dry according to direction.

2-3 servings

SHRIMP JUMBLE

Prepare and dry at home:
Saute: **4 strips bacon**
1/2 cup chopped onion
1/4 cup chopped green pepper
Drain on paper towels and blot to remove as much fat as possible.
Crumble bacon.
Combine with:
2 cups boiling water
3 tsp. instant chicken bouillon
1 can (1 lb. 12 oz.) whole tomatoes
2 cans water-packed shrimp, drained
1 cup uncooked rice
Pour into a greased 2-quart casserole. Bake uncovered at 375° for
45 minutes. Cool and dry according to directions.

3-4 servings

9

Sweets, Desserts and a Good Night

. . . Oh stars, show your light!
This fumbling storm clouded night
Needs to find its way . . .

Individual metabolism varies greatly. It depends on your physical condition and degree of exhaustion. When tired, eat some candy, drink some sugared lemonade, sip some hot sweet tea, have a few cookies. These quick calories will raise the blood sugar level and your spirits.

If it is a cold night, eat a candy bar just before crawling into your sleeping bag. You should sleep much warmer due to the increased blood sugar available for producing heat.

JIFFY CAMP CANDY

Prepare your favorite creamy frosting mix. Drop by teaspoonfuls on to a clean plastic bag or foil. Allow to set for an hour. Wrap extras in individual foil squares for trail energy.

HIKER'S ICE

Dissolve a fruit drink mix or cocoa mix in a little warm water. Add clean snow and stir till blended.

INSTANT PUDDINGS

At home: Combine the contents of a package of instant pudding with:

2/3 cup dry milk
1/3 cup coffee lightener

Seal in a Ziploc bag and label.

At camp: Add 2 cups cold water. Use a wire whip or a fork to beat until well blended (about 2 minutes). If possible, place in a cold stream or snow bank until set.

INSTANT RICE DESSERTS

Before adding the rice to water, add your choice of:

Diced unpeeled fresh apple
Diced dried fruit
Fruit leather
Raisins or dry banana flakes
Coconut or chopped nuts
Diced dried pineapple
Fruit drink crystals
Jello powder
Mint jelly or fresh crushed mint leaves
Fruit jam or marmalade
Red Hots (cinnamon candies)

RICE PUDDING

At home, combine:

1/2 cup instant rice
1/3 cup raisins

In another package, combine:

1 cup dry milk
1 pkg. (3-3/4 oz.) regular vanilla pudding mix

At camp: Combine 2-1/2 cups water, rice and raisins. Bring to a boil. Cover and simmer 4-5 minutes. Add the dry milk and pudding mix. Cook and stir over medium heat till thickened. Serve hot or cold.

Variations: Add cinnamon, coconut, chopped nuts, chocolate or butterscotch bits.

3-4 servings

LEMON PUDDING

At home, combine:
> **1 cup dry milk**
> **1 pkg. (3-3/4 oz.) instant lemon pudding mix**
> **1/4 cup toasted coconut (optional)**

At camp: Add dry ingredients to 2 cups cold water in a wide-mouth quart container with a tight lid. Shake vigorously for 30-40 seconds. Let stand 10-15 minutes to thicken. (If desired, stir the mixture with a wire whip in a bowl or cooking pot.)

2-3 servings

HOT NOG DESSERT

At home, combine:
> **4 tbls. dry instant vanilla pudding**
> **2/3 cup dry milk**
> **2 heaping teaspoons coffee lightener**
> **2 level tbls. flavored instant breakfast**

At camp: Add 2 cups hot water. Stir till dissolved.

2 servings

Spoon prepared instant vanilla pudding over sliced fruit cake for an easy dessert topping.

A doubled square of nylon net makes a good strainer when washing wild berries or wild greens.

Cranberry Desserts

Fresh cranberries are lightweight and full of vitamins. Cook a handful of cranberries with a little sugar and snipped dried fruit for a tangy dessert. (Try apples, prunes, or pears.)

CRANBERRY SAUCE

Combine in a saucepan:
1/2 cup sugar
1/2 cup water
1 cup fresh cranberries

Cook approximately 5 minutes or till the skins pop. Serve warm or chilled.

2 servings

CRAN-APPLE DESSERT

Simmer dry apple slices and a few fresh cranberries with some sugar, and enough water to barely cover. When the skins have popped on the cranberries, add a dash of cinnamon. Serve warm or chilled.

CRANBERRY WALLUP

Combine in a saucepan:
1/2 cup fresh, washed cranberries
1/2 cup dried apple slices, packed
1/4 cup raisins
1/4 cup sugar
1/4 tsp. salt
1-1/2 cups water

Simmer till apples are rehydrated and the cranberry skins have popped.

Add: **1/4 cup broken nuts**
2 tbls. orange juice crystals
1/2 cup miniature marshmallows
2 tsp. margarine

Stir till marshmallows and margarine have melted.

2-3 servings

FRUIT DESSERTS

CAMPER'S SHORTCAKE

Butter "skillet" toast and cut into small pieces in a bowl. Cover with wild cleaned chilled berries or fruit. Sprinkle with cinnamon sugar.

FRUIT COMPOTE

Combine:
> **Dry citrus pulp (or dry lemon crystals)**
> **Dry peach slices**
> **Dry strawberries**
> **Raisins**
> **Broken nuts**

Barely cover with water and allow to rehydrate. Add a dash of salt, some cinnamon and sugar to taste, and more water if needed.

Simmer till fruit is tender. Top with sour cream mix, if desired.

MELON SOUP

Rehydrate slices of dried honeydew, canteloupe, or other firm melon in a "juice" made with orange or grapefruit crystals. Use warm or cold water.

ALOHA FRITTERS

At home, combine:
    1 cup flour
    1 tsp. baking powder
    1 tsp. salt
    3 tbls. powdered whole egg
    1/3 cup dry milk
Also take:
    1 cup chopped dry fruit (pineapple, banana, apple,
       apricot, etc.)
At camp: Cover fruit with water to rehydrate. Combine dry batter ingredients with 1/2 cup water, including drained water from rehydrated fruit. Add 1 tbls. melted margarine. Stir till smooth. Fold in fruit. Drop by spoonfuls onto hot greased skillet. Turn to brown both sides.

Rehydrate dried fruits in Wyler's Fruit Punch Mix and hot water for a different taste. Try dried apple, pear, banana, peach, strawberry, fig.

HOT FRUIT SANDWICH

Rehydrate dried fruit by barely covering with water. Bring to a boil, cover, remove from heat. Let set 10-15 minutes.

Butter 2 slices of bread. Lay one slice buttered side down in a hot frying pan. Add a slice of cheese, then top with drained fruit.

Sprinkle with cinnamon sugar and top with the other slice of bread, buttered side up. Brown both sides.

CINNAMON APPLES

At home, combine:
    1 cup chopped dried apple slices
    1/4 cup raisins
    1/4 cup red cinnamon candies
At camp: Add water to barely cover, bring to a boil, cover and remove from heat. Let set 10-15 minutes. Return to stove and simmer till apples are tender and candies are mostly dissolved.

2-3 servings

STEWED FRUIT WITH NUTS

At home, combine:

1/2 cup pitted prunes, cut into small pieces
1/2 cup dried figs
1/4 cup dried apricots
1/4 cup raisins
2 tbls. blanched almonds
1 tbls. packed brown sugar
1/2 tsp. dried grated lemon peel or pulp

At camp: Cover with water and simmer till fruit is tender.

4 servings

Cookies

The following recipes are to be made up at home.

For something different, add flavored gelatin powder to oatmeal or sugar cookie recipes.

CARROT COOKIES

Cream together:

1 egg
1 cup shortening

Add: **2 cups flour**
4 tbls. brown sugar
1/2 tsp. salt

Combine thoroughly:

Add: **1 tsp. vanilla**
1 cup finely grated raw carrots
1 cup chopped nuts

Mix well.

Form into two 1" diameter rolls. Wrap in plastic film or waxed paper and chill 2-3 hours. Cut into 1/2" slices. Place on ungreased cookie sheets. Bake at 375° for 10 minutes. Cool on a wire rack. Freeze extra cookies for the next trip.

6 dozen

OATMEAL ROCKS

Cream together:
      1 cup shortening
      1-1/2 cups brown sugar, firmly packed
Add: **2 eggs and beat well**
Combine:
      2 cups flour
      1/2 tsp. salt
      1/2 tsp. baking soda
      2 tsp. baking powder
      2 tsp. cinnamon
Add to egg mixture alternately with:
      2/3 cup sour or buttermilk
Add: **1-1/2 cups rolled oats**
      1 cup raisins or chopped dates
      1 cup chopped nuts
Drop by teaspoonfuls on a greased cookie sheet. Bake at 350° for 12-15 minutes. Cool on a wire rack.

4 dozen

OATMEAL-SESAME COOKIES
(These are crisp and keep well)

Combine:
> 1/2 cup cooking oil
> 1 cup brown sugar
> 1 egg

Combine:
> 2 tbls. buttermilk or soured milk
> 1/2 cup cut-up raisins (use scissors)
> 3/4 cup sesame seeds
> 1-1/4 cups rolled oats

Add to egg mixture.

Combine thoroughly:
> 1-1/4 cup whole wheat flour
> 1/2 tsp. soda
> 1/4 tsp. salt
> 1/2 tsp. nutmeg
> 1 tsp. cinnamon

Add to other ingredients and mix well. Drop by spoonfuls on a greased cookie sheet. Flatten with a fork dipped in cold water, or a drinking glass bottom. Bake at 375° for 10-12 minutes or till browned.

NUGGET COOKIES

Cream:
> 1/2 cup margarine
> 1/2 cup brown sugar, firmly packed
> 1 tsp. vanilla

Add and mix well: **1 egg, beaten**

Sift together and add:
> 1 cup plus 3 tbls. whole wheat flour
> 1/2 tsp. soda
> 1/2 tsp. salt

Stir in: **1/3 cup hulled sunflower seeds**
> 2/3 cup butterscotch or chocolate bits

Drop by teaspoonfuls on an ungreased cookie sheet. Bake at 375° for 10-12 minutes.

4 dozen

MOLASSES COOKIES

Cream together:
1/2 cup shortening
1/2 cup brown sugar, firmly packed
Into a one-cup measure, pour:
1/2 cup hot water
1 tbls. vinegar
1/2 cup molasses
Add to shortening and sugar. Add **1 egg**, combine thoroughly.
Sift together:
2-1/2 cups flour
1/2 tsp. salt
1/4 tsp. baking soda
1 tsp. baking powder
1/2 tsp. ginger
1/2 tsp. cloves
1/4 tsp. cinnamon
Add to wet ingredients and mix well. Drop by teaspoonfuls on a greased cookie sheet. Bake at 350° for 12-15 minutes. Cool on wire racks.

(This dough may be chilled, rolled out on a floured board and cut into shapes if you prefer a flatter package.)
3 dozen

SUN-CHIP COOKIES

Cream together:
> **1/2 cup margarine**
> **1/2 cup brown sugar, firmly packed**

Add: **1 egg**
> **1/2 tsp. vanilla**

Combine separately:
> **1/2 cup whole wheat flour**
> **1/2 cup toasted wheat germ**
> **1/2 tsp. soda**
> **1/2 tsp. salt**

Mix until well blended.

Add: **1 pkg. (6 oz.) chocolate bits**
> **1/2 cup hulled unsalted sunflower seeds**
> **1/2 cup coconut shreds**

Drop by teaspoonfuls on a greased cookie sheet. Bake at 350° for 10-12 minutes. Cool on wire racks.

3 dozen

COCONUT COOKIES
(No-Bake)

In a saucepan, combine:
> **1/2 cup milk**
> **2 cups sugar**
> **6 tbls. cocoa**
> **1/2 cup margarine**

Bring to a full rolling boil.

Remove from heat and stir in:
> **3 cups quick oats**

Add: **1 cup shredded coconut**
> **1/3 cup chopped nuts**

Drop by teaspoonfuls on waxed paper to cool. Flatten if needed to pack better.

MOLASSES BARS
(No-Bake)

Combine all ingredients in a large bowl:
1/2 cup molasses
1 cup dry milk
1/2 cup peanut butter
1/2 cup raisins

Knead and add more dry milk, a little at a time, until the mixture is no longer sticky. It should resemble pie dough. Turn out on waxed paper. Flatten to 1/2" thickness. Cut into 1" x 2" bars. Wrap individually in foil or plastic wrap. Store in the refrigerator till ready to use.

DATE COOKIES

Combine and sift together:
1-1/4 cups flour
1/2 tsp. soda
1/4 tsp. baking powder
1/4 tsp. salt
1/4 tsp. cinnamon
1/8 tsp. nutmeg

In a large bowl, cream together:
1/4 cup margarine
3/4 cup brown sugar, firmly packed

Add: **1 egg**
1/2 tsp. vanilla
1/2 cup dairy sour cream

Add sifted dry ingredients, a little at a time.
Fold in:
2/3 cup chopped dates
1/2 cup chopped nuts

Drop by teaspoonfuls on a greased cookie sheet. Bake at 400° for 10-12 minutes. Cool on wire racks.

5 dozen

CAROB BARS

Combine thoroughly:
> **2 eggs**
> **3/4 cup carob powder (health food store)**
> **3/4 cup brown sugar, firmly packed**

Add: **1/3 cup melted margarine**
> **1 tsp. vanilla**

Mix together:
> **3/4 cup flour**
> **1/2 tsp. baking powder**
> **1/2 tsp. salt**

Add to wet ingredients and mix well. Stir in 1/2 cup hulled sunflower seeds. Pour into a greased 8 x 8 x 2" pan. Bake at 350° for 25-30 minutes. Cool and cut into squares. Wrap individually.

PEANUT BUTTER CARAMELS

In a bowl, combine:
> **3 cups Rice Krispies**
> **1 cup salted peanuts**

In a saucepan, combine:
> **1/2 cup sugar**
> **1/2 cup light corn syrup**

Cook, stirring constantly, till it comes to a full boil. Remove from heat.

Stir in: **1/2 cup peanut butter**
> **1/2 tsp. vanilla**

Immediately pour the hot syrup over the cereal mixture and stir gently to coat thoroughly. Smooth into a buttered 8 x 8 x 2" pan. Cool thoroughly, then cut into 2" bars.

16 bars

SURVIVAL BAR

This recipe contains 1,000 calories—enough survival food for one day. It may be consumed dry, or cooked with water. Add cut-up dried fruit and nuts for variety.

Combine in a large bowl:

3 cups quick-cooking oatmeal
2-1/2 cups dry milk
1 cup brown sugar

In a small pan, bring to a boil:

1 tbls. honey
1 tbls. water

Add: **1/2 pkg. (3 oz. size) lemon gelatin**

Dissolve the gelatin in the hot honey water. Combine with the dry ingredients, mixing well. Add more warm water, a little at a time, till the mixture is moist enough to mold. Pack into a greased foil-lined pan, and place in the oven turned to the lowest setting. If it is over 250° leave the door open a few inches. When dry, cut or break into 2" pieces. Wrap in foil and store in the freezer.

Dessert Breads

PEANUT BUTTER BREAD

Combine:

      2-1/4 cups flour
      3 tsp. baking powder
      1 tsp. salt
      1/2 cup sugar

Combine and add:

      1 cup milk
      2 eggs
      1 cup crunchy peanut butter
      1/2 cup raisins (optional)

Pour into a greased loaf pan. Bake at 350° for approximately 1 hour, or till a toothpick comes out of the center clean. Cool 10 minutes in the pan, turn out on a wire rack. Wrap and store in the refrigerator overnight after it is cold. Slice the next day when chilled.

1 loaf

GRAHAM FRUIT SQUARES

Beat together:

      2 eggs
      3/4 cup honey (room temperature)

Add: **1/2 cup flour**
      1/2 cup graham cracker crumbs
      1/4 tsp. salt

Combine thoroughly.

Add: **1 cup cut-up dried fruit (dates, figs, prunes, etc.)**
      1 cup chopped nuts (almonds, pecans, walnuts, etc.)

Pour into a greased and floured 8 x 8 x 2" pan. Bake at 350° for 40-45 minutes or till it tests done in the center. Cut into squares while warm. Cool on wire rack. (For easier handling: Line the baking pan with foil. Grease and flour the foil. When the squares are baked, lift them out of the pan with the foil edges . . . much easier to handle.)

16 bars

GRANOLA FRUIT BREAD

Cream together:
> **1/2 cup margarine**
> **3/4 cup brown sugar, firmly packed**
> **2 eggs**

Combine and add:
> **1-1/2 cups mashed ripe bananas (about 3)**
> **1 tbls. lemon juice**

Combine and add:
> **1-2/3 cups flour**
> **3 tsp. baking powder**
> **1/2 tsp. salt**

Fold in:
> **1-1/2 cups granola cereal**
> **1/4 cup pitted chopped dates**
> **1/4 cup raisins**
> **1/2 cup chopped nuts**

Spoon into a greased and floured 5 x 9" loaf pan. Bake at 350° for 1 hour or till a toothpick comes out of the center clean. Cool in the pan 10 minutes, then turn out on a wire rack. When cool, wrap and refrigerate overnight before slicing.

1 loaf

PRUNE BREAD

Cook 1 package prunes according to package directions. Drain and chop. Save juice.
Combine:

1-1/2 cups flour
1 cup sugar
1/2 tsp. salt
1 tsp. baking powder
1 tsp. baking soda
1 cup graham flour
1/2 cup broken walnuts

Combine and add:

1 egg
1 cup sour or buttermilk
1/2 cup prune juice
2 tbls. cooking oil
2/3 cup chopped cooked prunes

Mix ingredients thoroughly. Pour into a greased loaf pan. Bake at 350° for about 1 hour or till a toothpick comes out of the center clean. Cool on a wire rack. Wrap in plastic and store in the refrigerator overnight before slicing.

1 loaf

CRANBERRY-CHEESE BREAD

Cut 2 tablespoons of shortening into:

2 cups flour
1 cup sugar
1-1/2 tsp. baking powder
1/2 tsp. soda
1/2 tsp. salt
2 tsp. fresh grated orange peel

Squeeze the juice from one orange. Add water to the juice to measure 3/4 cup. Blend in with:

1-1/2 cups shredded cheddar cheese
1 egg, beaten

Fold in:

1 cup fresh, washed cranberries, halved
1/2 cup chopped walnuts

Bake in a greased 9 x 5 x 3" loaf pan. Bake at 350° for 60-70 minutes, or till a toothpick comes out of the center clean. Let loaf stand 8 hours or overnight before slicing.

1 loaf

Fruit Cakes

BACKPACKER FRUIT CAKE

Combine:
> **1/2 cup brown sugar, firmly packed**
> **1/2 cup margarine**
> **1 carton (12 oz.) whipped honey**
> **1 egg**
> **1 tsp. salt**

Combine and add:
> **1 cup whole wheat flour**
> **1/2 cup toasted wheat germ**
> **3/4 cup sunflower seeds, roasted**
> **1 pound raisins (or coarse-ground dried fruit)**
> **1 small pkg. chocolate chips**
> **1 small pkg. butterscotch chips**
> **2 cups chopped nuts**

Add 1/4 cup water if the mixture is too stiff. Spread evenly in 9" x 14" baking pan. Bake at 325° for 1-1/4 hours. Cool. Cut into 2" squares. Wrap individually in plastic wrap or foil.

DRIED-FRUIT CAKE

This easy-to-make fruit cake and a piece of sharp cheese makes a good breakfast or lunch.
Combine:

2 cups flour
1-1/2 cups sugar
2 tsp. baking powder
3/4 tsp. salt
1/2 cup orange juice crystals (Tang, Start)

Combine and add:

5 eggs, lightly beaten
1 tsp. vanilla
1/4 cup water

Add: **4 cups lightly packed dried fruit cut into 1/2" pieces**
       Choose 3 or more kinds from apple slices, apricots, figs,
       peaches, pears, pitted dates, raisins, etc.

Add: **3 cups whole almonds, pecan halves, walnut pieces, or a**
       mixture of nuts

Stir until the ingredients are well distributed. Spoon the mixture into four 6" x 3-1/2" foil or metal loaf pans which have been well greased and the bottoms lined with waxed paper.

Bake at 325° for 1-1/4 hours or till well browned. Turn out on a wire rack after they have set in the pans for 10 minutes. Peel off the waxed paper.

When completely cold, wrap airtight in plastic and refrigerate before slicing. This will keep well in the freezer for future trips.

References for Food Dehydration:

How To Dry Fruits and Vegetables At Home by Food Editors of Farm Journal, Doubleday & Co.
Home Canning-Preserving-Freezing-Drying, by editors of Sunset Magazine, Menlo Park, Calif. 94025.
College Extension Services: Washington State University and Utah State University.

Index

Haiku from Ideas by John Muir

Climb the mountains and
Get their good tidings. Cares will
Drop off like Fall leaves.

Nature's peace, storm's energy,
Wind's freshness, will flow in you
Like sun in tall trees.